Open Baptism

MARK DALBY

Open Baptism

SPCK

First published in Great Britain 1989
SPCK
Holy Trinity Church
Marylebone Road
London NW1 4DU

British Library Cataloguing in Publication Data

Dalby, Mark
Open baptism.
1. Church of England. Infant baptism
I. Title
265'.12

ISBN 0–281–04421–X

Phototypeset by Deltatype, Ellesmere Port, South Wirral
Printed in Great Britain by Hollen Street Press Ltd, Slough

Contents

1

Setting the Scene

I was visiting in the married quarters of an RAF station. I had had a message that some parents wanted their baby christened, and I was calling to make arrangements. Father was out, but mother was at home and very welcoming. She was also very honest. 'Of course, I'm not religious. I don't believe in God or anything like that. But we've got to have baby christened. I mean, if he died or anything and he'd not been christened he'd go to hell, wouldn't he?'

That was as confused a statement as any I have heard, but I have encountered plenty of other confusions about baptism, and so has every minister.

When I was a curate, Sunday afternoon baptisms at 3 were the norm, and there were always some families who wanted theirs to be the only baby baptized that day. If there was more than one, they'd ask, Could theirs be baptized separately, say at 4? Baptism was essentially a family occasion, their family occasion, and the presence of strangers would spoil it.

Then there was an inner-city parish. Parents who wanted a christening had to fill in a standard form which I inherited from my predecessor. Were they baptized and confirmed? Were the godparents baptized and confirmed? Baptisms were not very numerous, but in seven years I do not remember a single form in which every space was not ticked. It was a case of, 'If in doubt, say Yes'.

In my present parish there are many more baptisms, and we baptize nearly a hundred children each year. We try to take these baptisms seriously. We ask parents to make a personal application in church at a Sunday service. We ask them to attend a preparation meeting. We try to ensure that some of the godparents are properly qualified. At the same time we believe that a request for infant baptism should normally be granted, and granted gladly, and that our approach should be as open and generous as possible. A dozen or so times in nine years, when parents have found our requirements unacceptable and decided not to proceed with the baptism, we have been desperately sad. We want to say 'Yes'.

But many clergy nowadays feel that the requirements should be far more stringent, and that we should be saying 'No' far more often. Some say, 'Christian baptism only for the children of Christian parents'. Others say, 'Come to church for six months, and then we'll talk about the christening.' 'What you really want', they add, 'is not baptism for your baby but a simple service of thanksgiving.'

I can see the force of all this. Very few of the parents whose children I baptize are regular churchgoers. Sometimes one will say quite openly that he or she is not a believer in any sense. Sometimes it is clear that the real desire for the baptism comes not from the parents but from the grandparents. And almost always the gap between the Church's understanding of baptism and that of the parents is vast.

Obviously there are problems with the open approach. But these are the pastoral problems of ignorance and lack of commitment. The rigorous approach does nothing to solve these and merely creates the further problem of resentment. Quite apart from this, however – and this is my main contention – the open approach is well grounded in Scripture and tradition in a way that the rigorous one is not. Yet it is the rigorous approach which has been gaining ground lately. Revised baptism services have made increasing demands on parents, and a sincere and sustained campaign is being mounted against 'indiscriminate baptism'.

In 1982 the World Council of Churches issued a report, *Baptism, Eucharist and Ministry*, sometimes known for short as BEM. It recorded a remarkable measure of agreement between Churches of very different traditions. But it also noted areas of continuing disagreement. One of these was infant baptism, and especially 'indiscriminate baptism'. The report states that Churches which practise infant baptism

2

'must guard themselves against the practice of apparently indiscriminate baptism and take more seriously their responsibility for the nurture of baptized children to mature commitment to Christ'.[1]

My own view is that we are well aware of our responsibility for Christian nurture, though the difficulties are formidable and we still have a long way to go. But I am not at all convinced that 'apparently indiscriminate baptism' is wrong. On the contrary, I believe that it is the growing rigidity which presents the real danger both to the gospel and to the Church. But BEM has given a boost to the rigorists, and a new organization has been formed, The Movement for the Reform of Infant Baptism. Its first aim is 'to bring to an end the practice of indiscriminate baptism', and to achieve this it seeks 'the reform', i.e. the tightening, 'of Canon Law relating to baptism'. It already has a bishop as its president.

The Church of England is full of pressure groups, and some are very much on the fringe. But the tightening up of baptismal discipline has strong support in the General Synod. In 1986 an official of the Convocation of York claimed that the Synod had twice expressed its will 'to rule out indiscriminate baptism', and promised that an amendment to the canons would be proposed to give effect to this.[2] Later, in 1988, a private member's motion, supported by 122 other members, was moved to call attention to BEM's concern about 'apparent indiscriminate baptism'. It claimed that this concern was 'increasingly shared by many people of differing theological persuasions in the Church of England'.[3] I shall look at these statements and motions more closely later on. I quote them here only as evidence of the rigorist campaign now being mounted against 'indiscriminate baptism'.

Some of those involved in this campaign reject the label 'rigorist'. I use it of them myself only in default of any other. I gladly acknowledge that clergy who adopt a strict baptism policy may be very loving people and that their pastoral sincerity is beyond question. But I am not convinced by a recent suggestion that we should abandon talk of rigorism and speak instead of 'loving discernment'. To me this is merely the putting of a velvet glove on what remains an iron fist.

On the other hand, for my part I want to put a question against the term 'indiscriminate baptism'. History does not record who first used it. It might even have been meant as a compliment, and I know one clergyman who boasts of being 'rigorously indiscriminate'. After all, there is something scandalously indiscriminate about God himself: 'He makes his sun rise on the evil and on the good, and sends rain on the just and on the unjust' (Matt. 5.45). But as far back as 1896 Hensley Henson, later Bishop of Durham, declared that 'Indiscriminate baptizing is indecent in itself, discreditable to the Church, and highly injurious to religion'.[4] What Henson was actually describing was baptism administered carelessly with no preparation, no explanations, no questions, no demands and no follow-up. I doubt if anyone would defend that today. But, as Basil Moss has pointed out, 'indiscriminate baptism' does not necessarily imply that 'baptism is treated carelessly, or without efforts to instruct parents and godparents in the meaning of the rite, and the obligations it entails'. For him, it means 'baptizing the children of those who ask for it without applying any discriminatory tests or restrictive disciplines'. The real point, he says, is 'whether, in the end, when all that can be is said and done, baptism is actually refused, or is made so difficult that in effect it is refused'.[5]

Moss's comments are the most helpful that I know. But even these are not wholly satisfactory, for there is no such thing as absolutely indiscriminate baptism. If parents requested a baptism, but refused to bring their perfectly healthy child to church on Sunday and demanded that the vicar baptize it at home on Saturday afternoon because that would be more convenient for the family guests, I cannot imagine any vicar saying 'Yes'. There are particular times and places for baptism, and though there is some flexibility it is not unlimited. Again, no clergyman would stand outside the local supermarket and beg all parents who passed to let him baptize their babies. In practice we all discriminate in favour of those

4

infants for whom baptism is actually requested. It is not a matter of applying no 'discriminatory tests or restrictive disciplines', but rather of applying a minimum of such tests. It is not a matter of never refusing baptism under any circumstances, but rather of making the tests and disciplines sufficiently easy that anyone who genuinely wishes can fulfil them.

Absolutely indiscriminate baptism does not exist, and those who attack 'apparently indiscriminate baptism' are really attacking what has sometimes been called 'general baptism'[6] and what I would call 'open baptism'. But most modern writers reject even open baptism. They make infant baptism conditional on the faith of the parents, and a whole generation has been brought up to believe that this is the real teaching of the Church of England and that the open approach is an abuse. This is simply not true, and it is high time that the record was put straight. Open baptism is the traditional practise of the Church of England, and I believe that it should still be our practice today.

I am writing this book to commend open baptism. A comprehensive treatise on baptism, or even on infant baptism, would require something much longer, and if a Baptist reads this book I do not expect him to be converted by it. I am writing specifically for those who already believe in infant baptism in some sense. I want to commend the open approach to those who have never seriously considered it. And I want to reassure those (perhaps the majority) who still practise it (but sometimes with an uneasy conscience because they know how widely it is criticized). To do this, I put forward five propositions about infant baptism. Some are related more directly to the open approach, but all are consonant with it and ultimately supportive of it.

1. *Infant baptism should still be regarded as the norm here in England.* Many people nowadays speak of adult baptism as the norm, and of infant baptism as something exceptional which needs special justification. But adult baptism is the norm only where the gospel is preached for the first time. In England

5

infant baptism has been the norm for many centuries, and it is still the norm today.

2. *Infant baptism speaks not of original guilt but of God's prevenient grace*. Infant baptism has sometimes been commended largely as the means of saving the newborn child from hell, and there are traces of this even in our Prayer Book. We are right to reject this view, and it is better to see infant baptism in terms of the grace of God which goes before us at every stage of our lives, including infancy.

3. *Infant baptism should reflect the welcome which Jesus gave to the children*. This theme is prominent in the Prayer Book, though absent from our latest rites. But there are good grounds for linking the story of Jesus and the children with baptism, and it is significant that Jesus welcomed and received all the children who were brought to him.

4. *Infant baptism is administered in the faith of the Church*. There is a clear link in the New Testament between baptism and faith, but in infant baptism this faith is that of the Church as a whole and not just that of the parents. Believing parents are a great blessing, but they are not a prerequisite for baptism.

5. *Infant baptism looks forward to the child's growth as a Christian*. There can be no guarantees here and there are frequent disappointments. But we cannot abandon this hope. The Church requires qualified godparents not only to express her faith but also to help her children's growth. The less committed the parents are, the more important the god-parents' role becomes.

In expounding these propositions, as I do in the next five chapters, I look at the development of the Christian tradition from biblical times onwards and I sometimes dwell at length on Reformation and seventeenth-century controversies. At one time Anglican writers felt that their work was done if they could establish that theirs was the definitive Anglican position adopted once for all at some decisive point in the past. Those days have gone, and they will never return. Nonetheless many of the questions which concern us today were discussed very thoroughly in earlier times. People may well wish to amend the classical Anglican view, but at least they should know what it was and why it was.

In my later chapters I look more closely at some of the most recent developments, and also at the arguments for the restriction of baptism put forth in various Grove Booklets. Some of the recent developments represent a proper adaptation of our procedures to the pastoral conditions of the twentieth century, but others pose a deep threat to our tradition of open baptism. The Alternative Service Book, with its preference for adult baptism, its ignoring of Jesus and the children and its explicit demands on the parents, is particularly unfortunate here. ASB has enriched our worship in many ways, and I for one use it every day. But on baptism it lacks the openness of the Prayer Book, and the generation that knows only ASB and Grove is severely handicapped. Yet it would take only a very few amendments to improve ASB vastly, and I list these amendments in my final chapter.

NOTES

1. Faith and Order Paper No. 111 (Geneva World Council of Churches, 1982), p. 6.
2. General Synod, *Report of Proceedings* XVII (1986), 992–4.
3. ibid. XIX (1988), 1015.
4. 'The Administration of Holy Baptism in Large Urban Parishes', Sermon preached before the University of Oxford on 14 June 1896, reprinted in *Apostolic Christianity* (1898), p. 320.
5. *Crisis for Baptism*, ed. Basil S. Moss (London, SCM, 1965), p. 23.
6. cf. R. R. Osborn, *Forbid Them Not*, London, SPCK, 1972.

2
The Norm

Infant baptism should still be regarded as the norm here in England

Many of us who practise infant baptism believe that it was probably practised in New Testament times. The precedent of Jewish proselyte baptism, the parallel between baptism and circumcision (Col. 2.11f.), the Lord's welcome of the children (Matt. 19.13–15; Mark 10.13–16; Luke 18.15–17), the household baptisms in Acts (10.48; cf.11.14; 16.15 and 33; 18.8) and 1 Cor. (1.16), the holiness of believers' children (1 Cor. 7.14) and the status of children *within* the church (Eph. 6.1–3; Col. 3.20) – all these cumulatively are pointers to infant baptism. But we cannot be certain. From 1958 to 1962 the German scholars Jeremias and Aland re-examined all the possible evidence with meticulous care only to reach diametrically opposite conclusions.[1]

Whatever our own conclusions, most of us are happy to admit that adult baptism was the norm in New Testament times and that infant baptism was derivative, though it might be more accurate to speak of household baptism as the norm, without prejudice as to whether households included infants. But infant baptism is clearly attested by Tertullian (who disliked it), Hippolytus, Origen and Cyprian in the third century. There was a reaction against it in the middle of the fourth century, probably because of fear of the heinousness of post-baptismal sin, but it soon became common again. 'Common', but still not the norm. This is not to say that it was controversial; it was not. It is rather that in many areas the Church was still in a missionary situation where, as in New Testament times, adult or household baptism was the norm.

But as the borders of Christendom were enlarged, infant baptism did become the norm, and except for the occasional Jew everyone in the Middle Ages was baptized as an infant.

It was inevitable that in the first English Prayer Books in 1549 and 1552 the only baptismal provision was for infants. The form for the baptism of 'such as are of riper years' was not added till 1662, and then only because of 'the growth of Anabaptism' and 'for the baptizing of natives in our plantations, and others converted to the faith'. Infant baptism remained the norm, and it could hardly have been otherwise.

There is a modern tendency, however, to regard adult baptism as the norm. In 1946 Dom Gregory Dix complained, 'The Prayer Book treats Infant Baptism as the norm, and Adult Baptism as an occasional anomaly. That is to say, we take mediaevalism for granted.' He continued,

> The Church can very well afford Infant Baptism, even as the practice in the vast majority of cases (which it never was in pre-Nicene times) *provided that it is never allowed to be thought of as normal*, that it is regarded always as an abnormality, wholly incomplete by itself and absolutely needing completion by the gift of the Spirit and the conscious response of faith.[2]

So far we have been considering the Church's normal, i.e. usual, practice, and we have seen how in this sense infant baptism gradually replaced adult baptism. But Dix was thinking of the norm as the standard by which all variants must be judged, and the distinction has been brought out very clearly by the American Roman Catholic writer, Aidan Kavanagh:

> A *norm* in this sense has nothing to do with the number of times a thing is done, but it has everything to do with the standard according to which a thing is done . . . The normal as defined by tradition is differentiated from the usual as defined by convention.[3]

Dix insisted that adult baptism should always be regarded as the norm because infant initiation could never be complete. Full initiation included confirmation, which he understood as 'completion [of baptism] by the gift of the Spirit', and 'the conscious response of faith'. Confirmation could be given to infants as it had been in the past and as it still is in the Eastern Churches, but the conscious response of faith – which the primitive Church had required of adults before baptism and which the Church of England required of adolescents before confirmation – was impossible for infants.

Dix's emphases, though not all his nuances, gained immediate support and in 1948 a report on *The Theology of Christian Initiation* declared:

> It is not to be thought that the Baptism of Infants (defensible though we believe the practice to be) can bear the whole weight of theological meaning which the New Testament places upon the Initiation of Adults. The present-day counterpart to the primitive initiation is not baptism alone, but Baptism together with Confirmation, followed by First Communion.[4]

The 1948 Lambeth Conference accepted this view,[5] and the way was now clear for the Liturgical Commission in its 1958 report, *Baptism and Confirmation*, to provide new services which would give clearer expression to it. In its introduction the commission claimed boldly:

> In the New Testament Adult Baptism is the norm, and it is only in the light of this fact that the doctrine and practice of Baptism can be understood . . . The Baptism and Confirmation of Adults is treated as the archetypal service, and is printed first . . . Infant baptism is printed next, set out as a separate service.[6]

E. C. Whitaker, an eminent liturgist who was not then a member of the commission, defended this stance. In saying that adult baptism was the norm the commissioners had set out 'the inescapable truth', and their presentation of the services followed naturally from this:

> Logically we must begin with the rites of adult initiation as the archetype, of which the other rites can only be an adaptation, dependent upon the archetype as regards their theology and most probably as regards the liturgical presentation of that theology.[7]

For all this, however, the 1958 services were widely criticized, and even had they commended themselves there was no legal machinery by which they could have been authorized for use. But in 1965 this machinery was provided with the passing of the Prayer Book (Alternative and Other Services) Measure, and in 1966 the 1928 Baptism services were authorized as part of the Series One provisions. Here, as in 1662, infant baptism was normative, but in 1966–7 the Liturgical Commission produced another set of services in which Adult Baptism and Confirmation, followed by Communion, were again the archetype. Whitaker, now a member of the commission, admitted that the idea of adult baptism as the norm had been questioned, and he emphasized that 'This word "norm", which at best is not a beautiful one, does not appear in the 1967 report'. The theology of adult baptism and of infant baptism was one and the same, and it might have been thought that one order of service would have sufficed for both. But the circumstances of adult baptism enabled a fuller rite, while infant baptism called for modifications 'to accommodate it to the fact that the candidate is an infant and brought to baptism by sponsors'. Hence 'it is the adult rite which must be written first and then modified to accommodate the circumstances of infant baptism, rather than the other way round; and therefore it is placed first'.[8] The 1967 services were authorized in the following years as Series Two, and they are still in use today.

Whitaker agreed with Dix in regarding adult baptism as the norm, but he did not regard infant baptism as incomplete in the way that Dix did, and there now arose a reaction against some of the claims made concerning confirmation. In 1967 Evangelicals at their Keele Congress declared that 'Christian Initiation is sacramentally complete in Baptism',[9] and in 1971 the Ely report, *Christian Initiation: Birth and Growth in the Christian Society*, affirmed, 'Baptism cannot be added to, supplemented, or "completed". It is the one and complete sacrament of Christian initiation.'[10] In 1975 Whitaker himself wrote a booklet entitled *Sacramental Initiation Complete in Baptism*. Nonetheless, in 1977 the Liturgical Commission in its modern-language initiation services continued to treat the full adult rite of Baptism, Confirmation and Communion as the archetype. These 1977 services were authorized as Series Three in 1979, and they were incorporated with only minimal amendments into *The Alternative Service Book 1980*.

We can agree with the ASB provisions to some extent. Adults normally received baptism, confirmation and first communion together in the primitive rites, and ideally adult candidates should receive all three together today. We can agree too if the impression is given that infant initiation consisting only of baptism is less complete than the adult form – for despite the talk of 'sacramental initiation complete in baptism' initiation which does not culminate in communion must always be incomplete. In primitive times whenever infants were initiated at all they received everything that an adult received, confirmation and communion as well as baptism. The disintegration of the unified rite in the West was an accident of history. In the East all three are still administered to infants, and some Anglicans hope that this will one day be our own practice again. But to say that infant initiation today is incomplete does not mean that it is necessarily unsatisfactory, and the disintegration of the unified rite need not be regarded as a tragedy. Initiation is always a process rather than a single event, and for infants we can see it as a process which begins with baptism but is completed later with admission to communion after personal profession of faith and confirmation. On either view, infant baptism can still be regarded as the norm.

The real difficulty arises when the desire for a unified rite is linked with the desire for a personal profession of faith. If these two together are regarded as the norm, infant baptism becomes if not illegitimate at least highly abnormal. ASB does not adopt this view explicitly, but by presenting the full adult rite as the norm, the archetype, it does imply that infant baptism is a deviation from the norm, an exceptional thing; and if you want something exceptional the onus is on you to justify your request. Where infant baptism is regarded as the norm, no such justification is required, but ASB inevitably encourages the working out of criteria by which to assess the request, and the more one sees infant baptism as exceptional the more stringent the criteria become.

The American Episcopalian, A. Theodore Eastman, has warned that 'the suggestion that the baptism of adults is normative, both historically and theologically, may lead us down a slippery path', and that it is dangerous to imply that infant baptism is somehow abnormal.[11] This danger has already become apparent among Roman Catholics in the United States. The Roman Catholic Church issued a revised *Rite of Baptism for Children* in 1969, a revised *Rite of Confirmation* in 1971 and a new *Rite of Christian Initiation of Adults*, popularly known as RCIA, in 1972. The RCIA was an adaptation of the ancient catechumenate to the needs of a modern missionary church. It put forward a scheme for the initiation of new converts which could last several years, beginning with their admission to the catechumenate and reaching its climax with their receiving the three 'sacraments of Christian initiation'. Liturgists and pastors alike were excited by it. Quite unjustifiably, North American writers claimed the support of the Second Vatican Council in treating RCIA as the norm, and Kavanagh wrote unambiguously, 'It is clear that in the rites of initiation of adults we have, in fact, the definitive statement of what the Roman Catholic Church's *norm of baptism* is henceforth to be.'[12] All this led to a distressing disparagement of infant baptism, and in 1980 the Vatican had to issue an *Instruction on Infant Baptism* re-emphasizing that infant baptism was still 'a general rule' and 'a serious duty'.[13]

The clearest comment on this whole question of norms comes from A. R. Vidler:

> It is sometimes supposed that because Christian initiation was originally received only or mainly by adults, and it is doubtful whether in the New Testament there is reliable evidence of the initiation of children, therefore infant baptism, however justifiable, entails a departure from what must be theologically normative. But it is equally possible, and perhaps more reasonable, to regard the New Testament period as in this respect abnormal and exceptional. Not until families and nations were Christian could Christian initiation assume its normal form.[14]

Most of the Christians whom we encounter in the New Testament were first-generation Christians. But wherever the gospel is accepted and takes deep root, first-generation Christians eventually become a minority and the development of new initiatory patterns is inevitable. Vidler goes on to say, 'The Biblical testimony as a whole supplies no warrant for excluding children from church membership.' If we recognize this by baptizing them and even creating a new norm we are not being unfaithful to the Scriptures. For the greater part of its life the Church has done just this. Historically and theologically infant baptism has been its norm and standard.

Gordon Kuhrt has described the maxim that 'adult baptism is the norm' as 'one of those jumbo-statements that includes much truth but into which can be smuggled possibilities of confusion and error'. He goes on to say that 'in the Christian family adult baptism will be exceptional and infant baptism the norm'.[15] I agree with this, but would want to extend 'the Christian family' into 'the Christian country'. How far England today is a Christian country is, of course, debatable, and to form a precise judgement we would need to look separately at different regions and groups. Certainly Christendom as such is a thing of the past. Much of our work nowadays is mission work, and Kuhrt can reasonably argue that 'the western world is increasingly seen to be a largely secularized mission-field needing evangelism than part of a Christendom needing pastoral care'.[16] But though there is an obvious case for regarding the 1990s as a decade of evangelism, the situation is not as desperate as it sometimes seems. Those who claim to be Christian believers are far more numerous than the small company of regular Christian worshippers, and society is still permeated at many points by Christian standards and values.

Basil Moss has pointed out that 'The line people take about indiscriminate baptism seems to depend not a little on the assumptions made about society and the Church'.[17] It is not surprising therefore that Kuhrt, with his pessimism about contemporary society, is opposed to 'indiscriminate' baptism. We shall clearly have to look further at society and the Church later on, but to spend more time on it now would distract us. If we forget for a while the distinction between 'Christian family' and 'Christian country' and return to our starting point of the norm as the usual, whatever may be the case in the future the figures speak for themselves about the situation today. In 1985

14

there were 201,000 baptisms in the Church of England of infants under one year of age as against 38,000 other baptisms.[18] There is no wholly reliable way of calculating the ages of these 38,000 others, but there are good grounds for thinking that only a quarter or so were old enough to answer for themselves. This would make about 230,000 infant and child baptisms against 10,000 adolescent and adult baptisms.

For the past forty years the Church of England has been moving slowly but surely along Eastman's slippery path, and we are now increasingly isolated. We have already noticed the Roman Catholic re-emphasis of the 'general rule' and 'serious duty' of infant baptism. The Episcopal Church in the USA and the Anglican Church of Canada have produced single rites for adults and infants alike (though adults and older children are presented first). But *An Australian Prayer Book* of 1978 places infant baptism first, while the Church of Ireland's *Alternative Prayer Book 1984* includes only infant baptism. *The Methodist Service Book* of 1975 places infant baptism first, and so too does *The Book of Common Order* issued by the Church of Scotland in 1979. It is high time that the Church of England rejoined the main stream. Infant baptism should still be regarded as the norm – in both senses – here in England.

NOTES

1. J. Jeremias, *Infant Baptism in the First Four Centuries*, ET, London, SCM, 1960; K. Aland, *Did the Early Church Baptize Infants?*, ET, London, SCM, 1963; J. Jeremias, *The Origins of Infant Baptism*, ET, London, SCM, 1963.
2. *The Theology of Confirmation in Relation to Baptism* (Dacre, Westminster, 1946), pp. 28–31.
3. *The Shape of Baptism: The Rite of Christian Initiation* (New York, Pueblo, 1978), pp. 108f.
4. p. 12.
5. *The Lambeth Conference 1948*, Part II (Reports) (London, SPCK, 1948), p. 109.
6. *Baptism and Confirmation* (London, SPCK, 1959), p. x.
7. *The Proposed Services of Baptism and Confirmation Reconsidered* (London, SPCK, 1960), p. 57.
8. *The New Services 1967* (London, SPCK, 1967), pp. 23f.

9. *Keele '67*, ed. Philip Crowe (London, Falcon, 1967), p. 35.
10. GS 30, p. 27.
11. *The Baptizing Community* (Minneapolis, Seabury, 1982), p. 23.
12. 'The New Roman Rites of Adult Initiation', *Studia Liturgica* X (1974), p. 35; cf. also *The Shape of Baptism: The Rite of Christian Initiation*, pp. 102–25.
13. *Instruction of the Congregation for the Doctrine of the Faith on Infant Baptism* (London, Catholic Truth Society, 1980), pp. 9, 14.
14. *The Theology of F. D. Maurice* (London, 1948), p. 98.
15. *Believing in Baptism* (London, Mowbray, 1987), p. 137.
16. ibid., pp. 138f.
17. *Crisis for Baptism*, p. 31.
18. *1987 Church Statistics* (London, Central Board of Finance, 1987), p. 8.

3

The Necessity

Infant baptism speaks not of original guilt but of God's prevenient grace

N. P. Williams, in his classic study of *The Ideas of the Fall and of Original Sin*, refers to a woodcut of a baroque church which was prefixed to a 1700 edition of the works of St Augustine,

> On the right of the picture is the baptistery, where a bishop is plunging a naked infant into the font; this infant is evidently one of the elect, for the Holy Spirit is represented as a dove descending upon him in a stream of supernatural glory. Parents, sponsors, acolytes stand around in various attitudes of edification. On the left is the nave of the church; here another christening party is seen, suddenly halted with expressions and gestures of horror and dismay, just before the entrance to the baptistery: in their midst, a nurse holds the corpse of an infant, who was being brought to baptism, but has that very moment unexpectedly died (of convulsions, or what not) on the very verge of receiving the Sacrament of regeneration, and whose soul must therefore be presumed to have gone straight to hell, in virtue of original sin.

The picture is surmounted by a scroll with the inscription in Latin, 'One is taken, and another is left; for great is the grace of God and true is his justice.'[1]

It is probable that the practice of infant baptism preceded the doctrine of original sin, and that the doctrine was developed in part as an explanation of the practice. Adult baptism was closely connected with the remission of sins, and theologians naturally sought to relate this to infants as well. But from the proper doctrine of original sin (which we shall look at in a moment) there quickly developed the further doctrine of original guilt. It was agreed that Adam's fall had involved all his descendants in loss, but Augustine, reading 'in

17

whom all sinned' rather than 'because all sinned' in Romans
5.12, argued that there was a seminal identity. Every subsequent human being was 'in the loins' of Adam when he
sinned. He was therefore personally guilty of Adam's sin and
needed forgiveness of that sin. An infant could receive this
only through baptism, and without baptism he would go to
hell.

From now on, two things were mixed up: original guilt
which made an infant justly liable to condemnation, and
original sin which, quite apart from any guilt attaching to it,
was displeasing to God and must be removed if he was to enjoy
the eternal fellowship with God which we call salvation. The
medievals, though still holding to original guilt, gradually
abandoned Augustine's rigorism and developed the idea of a
limbo infantium for infants who died without baptism. They
distinguished this from hell, with its positive pains and
torments, but they also distinguished it from heaven with its
perfect enjoyment of God. Its infant inhabitants were not
punished as they would have been if guilty in the fullest sense,
and they lacked no good thing which was natural to man, but
they lacked God's gift of salvation which he bestowed on
infants only through the grace of baptism with its removal of
original sin. No one, not even 'innocent' infants, had a *right* to
this gift, for the gift to which we have a right is not really a gift
at all. It was God in his love and mercy who offered the gift by
virtue of the atonement made by Christ for all sin, and he
offered it through baptism. 'Baptism', wrote St Thomas,
'works through the power of the passion of Christ which is the
universal medicine of all sins', and again, 'Baptism opens the
gates of the kingdom of heaven to the baptized in that it
incorporates him into the passion of Christ and applies its
power to man'.[2] Baptism was easily available: the element of
water was universal, and even one who was himself unbaptized
could baptize in emergency if he intended what the Church
intended.[3] God could hardly have made baptism easier, and
there could be no excuse for its neglect.

The instinct behind limbo was a merciful one, but the idea
itself was subtle and speculative and it was of more interest to

theologians than to parish priests and their flock. Langland's words in *Piers Plowman* summed up the popular teaching succinctly, 'A child without baptism cannot be saved',[4] and in the last resort the theologians would have agreed with this.

Augustine was the most eminent of the Fathers, beloved as much by the Reformers as by the scholastics – and probably more so. But the Reformers could not make use of limbo to soften Augustine's harshness, since it lacked any scriptural support. At times therefore they appeared more rigid than the scholastics, and both the Thirty-Nine Articles and the 1662 Prayer Book still exude the feel of Augustine's rigorism and betray a continuing confusion between original guilt and original sin. There is the demand that infants should receive baptism very soon after their birth:

> The Curates of every Parish shall often admonish the people, that they defer not the Baptism of their Children longer than the first or second Sunday next after their birth, or other Holy-day falling between, unless upon a great and reasonable cause, to be approved by the Curate.

There is the statement that 'all men are conceived and born in sin', and the prayer for the child 'that he, being delivered from thy wrath, may be received into the ark of Christ's Church'. There is the description of a baptized child as one 'who being born in original sin, and in the wrath of God, is now, by the laver of Regeneration in Baptism, received into the number of the children of God'. There is the statement in the Catechism that the inward and spiritual grace of baptism is 'A death unto sin, and a new birth unto righteousness: for being by nature born in sin and children of wrath, we are hereby made the children of grace'. There is the reference in Article Two to the death of Christ as a sacrifice for original guilt as well as for all actual sins, and the statement in Article Nine on original sin that 'in every person born into this world, it deserveth God's wrath and damnation'. There is the rubric at the end of the baptism service that 'It is certain by God's Word, that Children which are baptized, dying before they commit actual sin, are undoubtedly saved'. Finally there is the rubric at the beginning of the burial service which forbids the office to be used 'for any that die unbaptized'.

In fact, from the time of the Reformation, the Church of England has never taught formally that unbaptized infants cannot be saved, nor have most of her divines taught this. In its original form in 1536 the rubric that 'children which are baptized . . . are undoubtedly saved' continued with the words 'or else not',[5] but these last words were omitted in 1549 and the rubric was retained partly to give positive assurance and partly to affirm that confirmation (now no longer available to infants) was not equally necessary. But anyone unaware of the historical background could easily assume that the rubric still implied 'or else not', and G. W. Hart has declared: 'This single rubric has inadvertently done more perhaps than anything else to encourage superstitious views about baptism'.[6] Taken at face value, which is the only way most people could take it, the Prayer Book implied the absolute necessity of baptism. No loving parent could take risks here, especially with infant mortality as high as it was, and no loving priest could deprive a child of salvation by deferring or refusing baptism. Folk religion dies hard. The words as words may not have been remembered, but their thrust as repeated over many generations has perpetuated the medieval view of baptism. Even today, fears about their unbaptized child's salvation persist in the minds of many parents and, if these are exaggerated, it is the Church as a whole and not the parents who are to blame.

But the Church today does not think of a new-born child as the object of God's wrath, or as one who is in some way guilty as a result of original sin. It is not on this ground that we commend an open approach to baptism, for as E. J. Bicknell wrote:

An infant is not in the least responsible for his share in a fallen humanity. He needs indeed the grace of God to counteract the perverting influences which have already begun to work upon his life, but God cannot be said in any sense to blame him for his present condition. Nor can we believe that infants are personally exposed to the wrath of God. All that we can assert is that God hates and condemns that condition of humanity which shuts men out from fellowship with Himself . . . God cannot condemn men for a state for which they are not accountable. Rather, as suffering from a disease of the soul which disqualifies them for the highest life, they are the objects of His pity and redeeming purposes.[7]

In rejecting original guilt here, Bicknell was careful not to reject original sin as well. The two are different, and original sin needs to be reinterpreted rather than rejected. William J. Bausch, an American Roman Catholic, describes it very well as

a collective term for the unmistakable fact that sin has indeed preceded every human being born into this world and has always done so as far as we can determine. The result is that we are all born into a spiritually deprived atmosphere, created by long traditions of sinning men . . . Original sin, then, is not so much a personal fault as the cumulative weight of evil that burdens every man because of a solidarity with mankind prior to his own sins.[8]

On this view original sin is something from which infants need to be freed more than cleansed, and significantly the only prayer in the revised Roman Catholic rite which mentions original sin asks simply that God will 'set them free' from it.

Bausch goes on to explain that 'Baptism takes the infant and the adult from the solidarity of sin and places them in the solidarity of being in grace with Christ', and another Roman Catholic writer describes baptismal grace as the acceptance of the infant 'into a community of people living in reversal of the sinful orientation which constitutes original sin'.[9] Within this community the reality of forgiveness is experienced daily, and this has consequences not only for the healing of original sin but also for the forgiveness of actual sins. Thus the Methodist Geoffrey Wainwright asks:

May not, therefore, the baptism of an infant be seen, even where there is a refusal to attach the categories of sin and guilt to the infant's solidarity with the human race 'in Adam', as the proleptic remission, for Christ's sake, of the actual and culpable sins which the person will commit when at an age of responsibility he deliberately makes Adam's sin his own (as he certainly will)?[10]

Infant baptism here is truly 'for the remission of sins', and it is salvation not only in the sense of being saved from hell or limbo but also in the deeper sense of being brought by the grace of God to new possibilities of wholeness in the Body of Christ.

But we must still remember, as Bicknell pointed out, that original sin impedes our fellowship with God from the very beginning of our lives, and if we think of salvation in terms of this fellowship we cannot speak glibly of the salvation of unbaptized infants (or of anyone else) as if this was their right and not God's gift. In 1893 a Roman Catholic book was placed on the Index for suggesting that unbaptized infants might attain a more exalted state than limbo,[11] and as recently as 1954–5 there was a series of learned articles in *The Clergy Review* reaffirming their necessary exclusion from heaven.[12] But in 1961 there was published a book entitled *From Limbo to Heaven*,[13] and that title is indicative of the way in which Roman Catholic teaching has moved. Whatever the precise status of limbo in the Roman Church at the moment, it seems that unbaptized babies have been removed from it *en masse*. Similarly, baptism is no longer ordered 'at the earliest opportunity' but simply 'within the first weeks after birth'. The 1980 Vatican *Instruction* says clearly that the Church 'knows no other way apart from baptism for ensuring children's entry into eternal happiness'.[14] But the keyword here is 'knows'. God is not bound by the sacraments, and the *Instruction* does not rule out that God himself may know what the Church does not.

ASB states that when parents request emergency baptism for an infant 'they should be assured that questions of ultimate salvation . . . for an infant who dies do not depend upon whether or not he had been baptised'. It is unfortunate that this new rubric loses not only the *prima facie* negative implication of its Prayer Book predecessor but also its note of positive assurance. None the less ASB is clearly right to imply that there are other considerations than baptism here. The main considerations are the nature of God and his will to save, and the great majority of writers of all schools believe that these lead inescapably to the conclusion that all infants will be saved, or at least have the opportunity of salvation.[15] But we must not lazily and casually presume on the mercy of God. He may save without baptism, but he has instituted and ordered it, and knowing this we have no alternative but to seek it: 'If God does give grace where the sacrament itself cannot be received, the sacrament remains necessary in cases where there is a possibility of receiving it'.[16]

But if original sin does not imply guilt, and if God can save without baptism, why should baptism be so necessary? The question is an old one. The Eastern Church has never had such a precise understanding of original sin as the Western Church, and centuries ago when St John Chrysostom was waxing eloquent on the blessings of baptism, he proclaimed:

> Blessed be God, who alone does wonderful things! You have seen how numerous are the gifts of baptism. Although many men think that the only gift it confers is the remission of sins, we have counted its honours to the number of ten. It is on this account that we baptize even infants, although they are sinless, that they may be given the further gifts of sanctification, justice, filial adoption, and inheritance, that they may be brothers and members of Christ, and become dwelling places for the Spirit.[17]

The Prayer Book also has a positive note, and it attributes the necessity of baptism not only to the need for cleansing from original sin, which we have already noticed, but also to the Lord's statement to Nicodemus, 'Unless one is born of water and the Spirit, he cannot enter the kingdom of God' (John 3.5). For the first thousand years – and more – of the Church's history, it never occurred to anyone to interpret these words as referring to anything other than baptism, and the Prayer Book is wholly traditional here. Quite apart from its exaggerated notions of original guilt, it teaches that the world into which the child is born is tragically separate from God. He needs to be born again in Christ, and into the new world which derives from him and is indwelt by his Spirit. 'If any one is in Christ', wrote St Paul, 'he is a new creation; the old has passed away, behold, the new has come' (2 Cor. 5.17). It is at baptism, teaches the Prayer Book, that this new birth, this new creation, takes place, and that the child is brought into a new relationship with God. He is made, in the words of the catechism, 'a member of Christ, the child of God, and an inheritor of the kingdom of heaven'. The necessity of baptism, therefore, is the necessity of the new birth. It should be administered as generously as possible, and received as quickly as possible.

The last paragraph represents a traditional answer, but a more radical one was put forward in the last century by F. D. Maurice. Maurice, like the traditionalists, believed that 'Baptism is a sacrament, grounded upon the atonement made for mankind by Christ',[18] but for him that atonement has already done for us what in traditional thinking is done for us at baptism. According to Maurice, mankind has already been taken into communion with the ascended Christ, the universal head of humanity, and every man is related to Christ, whether conscious of the relationship or not. The Church is the society in which this is acknowledged and believed. Its outward signs bear witness to our true state, and baptism, the first of these signs, is the enacted proclamation and assertion that what is true for mankind as a whole is true for this particular infant.[19] 'Baptism tells me that I am God's child',[20] he declared, and again:

> We tell all men, those who are most incredulous of our message, most hostile to it, that this Name is about them, that they are living, moving, having their being in it. They do not acquire this privilege by baptism; we baptise them because they have it.[21]

A strength of Maurice's view is that there is no problem about the fate of the unbaptized, 'Our baptism is the simplest and fullest witness of a redemption which covers and comprehends those who are not baptised'.[22] Its main weakness is that it allows baptism to assert something but not really to accomplish anything, and it does not seem to do justice to the Catechism's assertion that in baptism we are *made* the children of God. Maurice was aware of this criticism,[23] but it was his contemporary, F. W. Robertson, who provided the best answer to it:

> Coronation makes a sovereign; but, paradoxical as it may seem, it can only *make* a sovereign one who is sovereign already. Crown a pretender, that coronation will not create a king. Coronation is the

authoritative act of the nation declaring a fact which was fact before . . . Baptism makes a child of God in the sense in which coronation makes a king. And baptism naturally stands in Scripture for the title of regeneration and the moment of it.[24]

There are similarities between Maurice's view and that expressed in our own century by the Reformed theologian, Oscar Cullmann, with his stress on the 'general baptism' accomplished by Christ on Calvary,[25] but all we need to note now is that, if Maurice's view is preferred to the more traditional one, baptism is still necessary in that what is true must be recognized. Indeed, for Maurice salvation seems to consist precisely in this recognition of our status before God. This status is ours from the very beginning, and therefore baptism should be administered at the very beginning:

> Infant Baptism . . . has been a witness for the Son of Man and the universality of His kingdom, like no other. It has taught parents that to bring children into the world is not a horrible crime. It has led them to see Christ and His redemption of humanity through all the mists of our teachings and our qualifications. It has explained the nature of His Kingdom to the hearts of the poorest. Christ has been preached at the fonts, when we have been darkening counsel in pulpits.[26]

Moreover this status belongs to everyone, and therefore baptism should be administered without restriction to all for whom it is sought:

> We want to have this name, 'Child of God', marked upon each infant before he can speak or think or know what it means . . . We want it to be wrought so into our confessions that we shall feel our sin consists in forgetting it, that we are only delivered from our sin by remembering it.[27]

'What God has done' was the emphasis of Maurice. 'What God is doing' is the emphasis of the tradition. But in either case the emphasis is on God, and so it must always be in a true theology of baptism. The 1948 report on *The Theology of Christian Initiation* stated that infant baptism 'has particular importance as declaring the priority of God's act in the salvation and sanctification of His people'.[28] The 1980 Vatican *Instruction* describes infant baptism as 'truly evangelical, since it has the force of witness, manifesting God's initiative and the gratuitous character of the love with which he surrounds our lives: "not that we loved God but that he loved us . . . We love, because he first loved us"' (1 John 4.10, 19). It also speaks of baptism as 'the sign and means of God's prevenient love'.[29] All this is movingly expressed by Bausch,

> Basically the justification for infant baptism rests on the initiative of God Himself . . . It is God who reaches out to man, who forgives sins, who makes holy. God's activity (grace) is a free act. No one can earn it. God is master of His gifts. Man does not deserve them and cannot earn them. Any notion, therefore, that the good deeds or the faith of any human being *must* precede God's action, his grace-filled activity, in order for God to act, would imply curtailing God's power. He loves us when we do not deserve it. He shows mercy when we have no right to expect it and compassion when we did not think it was possible . . . It is on this biblical understanding of a God who is master of his gifts and who 'first loved us' that the reaching out in baptism to an infant is justified. It is the emphasis of a Godward approach. It is a recognition that God loves everyone who is born into his world prior to and apart from sin.[30]

The Methodist writer, W. D. Stacey, expresses himself similarly:

> In baptism God gives Himself to the child and also claims the child for His own. Just as the creation of physical life remains an act of sovereign love, though it cannot possibly meet with immediate, grateful response, so the initiation of spiritual life is unaffected by the inability of the child to respond.

God's action is neither conditioned by our responses nor dependent upon anything that may happen in the future: 'He establishes the relationship. He makes the promise.'[31]

Original guilt is a fiction. Original sin is a fact, and there is a universality about it just as there is about actual sin. But God's prevenient grace is also universal, for 'where sin increased, grace abounded all the more, so that, as sin reigned in death, grace also might reign through righteousness to eternal life through Jesus Christ our Lord' (Rom. 5.20f.). Infant baptism speaks not of original guilt but of God's prevenient grace.

The Necessity

NOTES

1. (London, Longman, 1929), p. 377. I owe this quotation to B. S. Moss, ed., *Crisis for Baptism* (London, SCM, 1965), pp. 34f.
2. *Summa Theologiae* 3:69:2 and 3:69:7, ET J. J. Cunningham (London, Eyre and Spottiswoode, 1975), pp. 125, 143.
3. ibid., 3:67:6, p. 69.
4. xi.82, ed. J. F. Goodridge (London, 1959), p. 167.
5. *Formularies of Faith*, ed. C. Lloyd (Oxford 1825), p. 7.
6. *Right to Baptize* (London, Hodder, 1966), p. 47.
7. 'Sin and the Fall', in *Essays Catholic and Critical*, ed. E. G. Selwyn (London, SPCK, 3rd edn 1929), pp. 223f.
8. *A New Look at the Sacraments* (rev. edn Cork, Mercier, 1983), p. 87.
9. I have mislaid the source of this quotation; my apologies to the writer.
10. *Christian Initiation* (London, Lutterworth, 1969), p. 26.
11. cf. A. Kavanagh, *The Shape of Baptism: The Rite of Christian Initiation*, (New York, 1978), p. 89.
12. Bernard Leeming, 'Is their Baptism really necessary?', *The Clergy Review* XXXIX (1954), pp. 66–85, 193–212, 321–40; XL (1955), pp. 129–151.
13. By Vincent Wilkin, London, Sheed and Ward, 1961.
14. p. 8.
15. cf. from the Roman Catholic tradition Lorna Brockett, *The Theology of Baptism* (Cork, Mercier, 1971), pp. 82–6; Aidan Kavanagh, *The Shape of Baptism*, pp. 89–97; W. J. Bausch, *A New Look at the Sacraments*, pp. 86–9; cf. from the Evangelical tradition John Inchley, *All about Children* (London, Coverdale House, 1976), pp. 13–30, 89–96; Geoffrey W. Bromiley, *Children of Promise* (Edinburgh, T. & T. Clark, 1979), pp. 91–104.
16. Lorna Brockett, *The Theology of Baptism*, p. 86.
17. *Baptismal Instructions* iii.6, ET Paul W. Harkins (New York 1963), p. 57.
18. *The Kingdom of Christ* (1st edn 1838), 1:115.
19. This summary is drawn from A. R. Vidler, *The Theology of F. D. Maurice*, p. 100. Vidler contains the fullest account of Maurice's teaching on baptism, but see also P. J. Jagger, 'Baptism in the Kingdom of Christ', *Faith and Unity* XVI (1972), pp. 52–6.
20. F. Maurice, *The Life of Frederick Denison Maurice* (1884), 2:242.
21. *The Conflict of Good and Evil in our Day* (1865), p. 179.
22. 'The Revision of the Prayer Book and the Act of Uniformity',

Macmillan's Magazine (April 1860), p. 424, cited Vidler, *The Theology of F. D. Maurice*, p. 111.

23. F. Maurice, *The Life of F. D. Maurice*, 2:271–5; cf. also A. M. Ramsey, *F. D. Maurice and the Conflicts of Modern Theology* (Cambridge University Press, 1951), pp. 35f.
24. *Sermons on Christian Doctrine* (London, J. M. Dent, Everyman edn, 1906), pp. 19f.
25. cf. *Baptism in the New Testament*, ET, London, SCM, 1950.
26. *The Gospel of the Kingdom of Heaven* (1864), p. 282.
27. *The Faith of the Liturgy and the Doctrine of the Thirty-Nine Articles* (1860), p. 13.
28. p. 21.
29. pp. 13f.
30. *A New Look at the Sacraments*, pp. 69f.
31. 'Indiscriminate Baptism', *London Quarterly and Holborn Review* (1961), p. 187.

4

Jesus and the Children

Infant baptism should reflect the welcome which Jesus gave to the children

I once attended a Methodist baptism service in Tonga, and I was delighted to find that one of the hymns sung was the Victorian evangelical favourite, 'When mothers of Salem their children brought to Jesus'. A Baptist might query the use of that hymn at a baptism, but many modern liturgists would wince at it. In some circles nowadays it is deemed almost axiomatic that the gospel story of Jesus welcoming the children (Matt. 19.13–15; Mark 10.13–16; Luke 18.15–17) has nothing whatever to do with baptism, and C. E. Pocknee has written: 'The reading of this lection at the font in direct connexion with infant baptism has done more than anything else to engulf Christian initiation in false sentimentality, and to obscure the true meaning of baptism.'[1]

The three synoptic versions of the story have slight differences, and it is worth printing all three in parallel:

Mark	*Matthew*	*Luke*
And they were bringing children to him, that he might touch them; and the disciples rebuked them. But when Jesus saw it he was indignant, and said to them, 'Let the children come to me, do not hinder them; for to such belongs the kingdom of God. Truly, I say to you, whoever does not	Then children were brought to him that he might lay his hands on them and pray. The disciples rebuked the people; but Jesus said, 'Let the children come to me, and do not hinder them; for to such belongs the kingdom of heaven.'	Now they were bringing even infants to him that he might touch them; and when the disciples saw it, they rebuked them. But Jesus called them to him, saying, 'Let the children come to me, and do not hinder them; for to such belongs the kingdom of God. Truly, I say to

29

Mark	Matthew	Luke
receive the kingdom of God like a child shall not enter it.'		you, whoever does not receive the kingdom of God like a child shall not enter it.'
And he took them in his arms and blessed them, laying his hands upon them.	And he laid his hands on them and went away.	

Those who brought the children are generally assumed to have been their mothers, and they have certainly become mothers in the popular retelling of the story just as Matthew's wise men have become kings. But the disciples' rebuke is addressed to the masculine *aùtois* which suggests either fathers or, as in Luke 2.27, both parents together. Yet neither fathers nor parents are mentioned explicitly, and some writers have suggested older brothers and sisters. All we can say for certain is that those who brought the children included males of some kind.[2]

The children too are not clearly defined. In Mark and Matthew and at two points in Luke they are *paidia*, a general word which modern versions more accurately translate as 'children' as against the Authorised Version's 'little children'. But Luke also writes of them as *brephē*, 'infants' or 'babes', and in all three Gospels they do not come of their own volition but are brought by others. That the Lord welcomes them is clear beyond question, but the words 'to such belongs the kingdom of God' are not as straightforward as they seem and there are a number of different interpretations:

(a) The kingdom belongs only to those whose whole life is a Day of Atonement, a becoming small before God. This is the interpretation of Jeremias who places the incident on the evening of the Day of Atonement.

(b) The kingdom belongs to children because, being young, they 'will not taste death before they see that the kingdom of God has come with power' (cf. Mark 9.1).

(c) The kingdom belongs to children and those like them because of e.g. their loving and trustful responsiveness, their dependence and poverty of spirit (cf. Matt. 5.3), their freedom from adult scepticism.

(d) The kingdom belongs to such children not because of any special spiritual qualities they possess as children but because they have been brought to Jesus.[3]

For our purposes, however, the precise interpretation is irrelevant. Jesus could not have said 'To such belongs the kingdom of God' if he had deemed them unqualified for the sacrament of initiation into that kingdom. This is not to say that Jesus actually had baptism in mind when he uttered the words. It is rather to say that the development of infant baptism was in accordance with his mind. But it is quite possible that the evangelists had baptism in mind, and several commentators have suggested that they used the narrative deliberately to answer questions which were then being raised about infant baptism.[4]

There are two other indications of a legitimate baptismal interpretation. First there is the Matthaean parallel (18.3) to Mark 10.15 and Luke 18.16, 'Truly, I say to you, unless you turn and become like children, you will never enter the kingdom of heaven.' Jeremias compares these three verses with the baptismal reference in John 3.5, 'Truly, truly, I say to you, unless one is born anew, he cannot see the kingdom of God.' He points out that in each case the saying is introduced by 'Truly, I say to you', there is a negative condition about receiving the kingdom like a child or being born anew, and there is a warning that otherwise one cannot enter or see it. For Aland 'the external parallelism of the words is but apparent', yet he admits that 'both sayings, despite their difference, have a common root in a dominical utterance'.[5]

Secondly, there are the words in all three Gospels, 'Do not forbid (*kōluete*) them'. Cullmann has pointed out that the verb *kōluein* is used in a specifically baptismal context four times in the New Testament (Matt. 3.13; Acts 8.36; 10.47; 11.17) and he has built up a strong case for arguing that it featured regularly in the earliest baptismal liturgy.[6] If this is correct, the use of the word by each of the synoptists would be a strong indication that they saw the story as relevant to baptism. It should also be noted that in Mark Jesus laid his hands on the children, and that in Matthew the children are brought explicitly 'that he might lay his hands on them and pray'. Such laying on of hands was also closely associated with baptism (cf. Acts 8.14–17; 19.5f.; Heb. 6.2).

It is certain that 'Forbid them not' was being applied to infant baptism when Tertullian wrote his *De Baptismo c*.206,[7] and by the eighth century when infant baptism was well established as the norm all three versions of the story had found a place in the liturgy. They were read during the ceremonies of the catechumenate, the Matthaean version on Lent III, the Marcan on Lent IV and the Lucan on Lent V.[8] But Easter baptism was already yielding place to instant baptism. In the later medieval rites the making of a catechumen was reduced to a brief ceremony in the church porch immediately before baptism proper. The three lessons were reduced to one, and in the Sarum rite the Mathaean version was used.[9]

The medievals wrote comparatively little about infant baptism as such since it was not a matter of controversy, but the rise of the Anabaptists at the Reformation brought the subject to the fore again. The great continental Reformers – Luther, Zwingli, Bucer, Calvin and Bullinger[10] – all saw the gospel story as justifying infant baptism, as did the Roman Catholics in the *Catechism of the Council of Trent*.[11] In England Archbishop Cranmer interpreted it similarly,[12] and he included it in its Marcan form in the 1549 Prayer Book. The formal distinction between the making of a catechumen and baptism proper was abolished, but the first part of the rite still took place 'at the church door' and the lesson was still read here. In 1552, however, the whole service took place at the font, and the lesson was now unambiguously baptismal in context. It remained so in 1662, 1928 and Series One.

The first official proposal for change came in the Liturgical Commission's 1958 rite. The commissioners explained:

In the Baptism of Infants, the Lord's command to his apostles to go and make disciples and to baptize them (Matt. 28.18–20) is substituted for our Lord's taking little children into his arms and laying his hands upon them and blessing them (Mark 10.13–16). This passage has no obvious connection with Baptism, and we have therefore substituted the Lord's command to baptize all nations.[13]

The claim that the passage 'has no obvious connection' with baptism was a strange one. The contrary views of Cullmann and Jeremias were widely known at the time, and for more than four hundred years the connection had been accepted as extremely obvious. It is not surprising that the substitution met with a 'sour reception'. Whitaker admitted this, but he went on to defend it on the ground that it was good for the parish priest to be able to point to the new passage 'and declare that we baptize, not because it is a pretty thing to do, not because someone thought it would be "nice", but in obedience to our Lord's command'.[14] But this was a poor criticism of the Prayer Book rite where baptism is grounded very firmly in the Lord's words in John 3 about the necessity of a new birth 'of water and the Holy Ghost'. It is only after this that the story of the Lord's welcoming the children is read.

E. C. Ratcliff, then the country's leading liturgist, now added his weight to the attack: 'A mist of sentimentality has collected around the passage, so that its irrelevance to baptism of children has been disregarded, and the nature of its connexion with baptismal rites has been overlooked.' He recounted the history of its liturgical usage, and continued:

The uninstructed person of to-day, ignorant of these matters and unlikely to be sentimental, might be pardoned if, hearing this passage read, he were led to wonder why, in order to 'christen' a child, the less convenient practice of baptizing him with water came to be preferred to the simple benedictory handlaying performed by Jesus and described in the lesson.

In a modern service, he concluded, designed with the uninstructed in view, the gospel lesson should offer a rationale of the sacrament being administered.[15]

Our criticisms of Whitaker apply equally to Ratcliff, and to speak of the 'irrelevance' of the passage was far more irresponsible than to deny its *obvious* connection'. As for his other arguments, he seems first to deplore popular sentimentality and then to deny it, and since the new rites were considerably more complex than the old, 'the uninstructed' – who were at least aware that baptism involved water – would have been the last group to appreciate them.

Happily the Lord's welcome of the children was restored, though not with its traditional prominence, in the Liturgical Commission's 1967 proposals, and it still features in the Series Two service which resulted from these. In 1971, however, a report was issued by the Doctrine Commission on *Baptism Thanksgiving and Blessing*. Many people had been suggesting that there should be a service of thanksgiving and/or blessing as an alternative to infant baptism in some cases. The Doctrine Commission was not unsympathetic to this provided that such a service was available for general use and was not regarded as a substitute for baptism. They suggested:

> Although Mark 10.13ff. was used in a baptismal context from the middle of the second century, there is no mention of Baptism in the original context, and it might perhaps be used here for its illustrative value. In the first place, Jesus showed a welcoming attitude towards children who had no claim on him and whose parents, it seems, entered into no obligations. Second, he rebuked his disciples who thought this inappropriate. Third, he took the opportunity to explain what entry into the Kingdom meant and its preconditions; and finally he blessed them.[16]

This gave some members of the Liturgical Commission exactly the opportunity they were looking for. In 1975 the Commission issued its first modern-language service for infant baptism and explained that it had retained all the elements of the Series Two introduction except for the story of the Lord blessing the children. It continued:

> Apart from the difficulties felt by some scholars in accepting that this story has any connection with baptism, we believe that it will be very appropriate in a service for the Blessing of Infants, if such a service is required by the Church.

Its only concession was to include the story among four possible gospel readings which might be used if infant baptism was administered at Holy Communion or at Morning and Evening Prayer.[17]

In 1977 the Liturgical Commission issued fuller proposals. Matthew 19.13–15 now appeared in the service of Thanksgiving for the Birth of a Child and also in the service of Thanksgiving after Adoption, but there was no change in the provisions for baptism.[18] The General Synod's Revision Committee then made matters even worse, and 'deleted from the *lessons* Mark 10.13–16, which we consider to be more appropriate in a service of Thanksgiving'.[19] This meant that in Series Three, which was authorized in 1979, the Lord's welcome of the children was wholly divorced from baptism. This divorce is perpetuated in ASB, and the authoritative commentary on ASB by R. C. D. Jasper and P. F. Bradshaw states simply that it is 'generally recognised as not referring to Baptism'[20] – though it must refer apparently to Thanksgiving for the Birth of a Child, Thanksgiving after Adoption and the Funeral of a Child since on each of these occasions it is still read!

Liturgical purists argue that the story was originally read not in the infant baptism service as such but at the making of a catechumen which preceded it and at which it was linked with a laying on of hands. Here, they say, it was perfectly appropriate just as it would be at a Baptist Dedication Service. It is not its use as such to which they object (it is after all a gospel story), but only its use in a baptismal setting. They can also argue, and rightly, that there is only one baptism, that the ultimate warrant for infant baptism must be the same as that for adult baptism, and that this must be sought in the Lord's own baptism, his words to Nicodemus or his command in the great commission. But no one denies this. The story of Jesus and the children can be related to baptism only if baptism as such is grounded elsewhere. But since it *is* grounded elsewhere, it is not out of place to use the story to show that it may properly be administered to children.

The purists' dislike of the story in a baptismal setting can best be understood in the light of their conviction that adult baptism is the norm. The equal distaste for it of many modern Evangelicals is *prima facie* more puzzling. Until recently Evangelicals were happy to continue the Reformers' use of it, and the great Bishop Ryle's comment was simple, 'A direct argument in favour of infant baptism the passage certainly is not. But a stronger indirect testimony it seems to me impossible to conceive.'[21] J. A. Motyer, Geoffrey Hart and Michael Green still make use of the story,[22] but Colin Buchanan has consistently taken a different view. In his first booklet on infant baptism, published in 1972, he wrote, 'There is of course no reliance placed upon Mark 10.13–16, etc. for this purpose,[23] and he subsequently criticized Cranmer for his mistake in attempting a justification of infant baptism in the course of the service, 'a mistake a hundred times compounded by his attempting to make the pedobaptist case from Mark 10.13–16!'.[24]

It may be, however, that there is a simple explanation for this volte-face. Many Evangelicals nowadays are fighting on two fronts: *for* infant baptism against Baptists and the house-church movement, and *against* indiscriminate baptism as practised by some of their fellow Anglicans. When infant baptism as such was their main concern, the traditional emphasis on Mark 10 was very useful, but now that indiscriminate baptism is an equal concern, Mark 10 has become an embarrassment, for Jesus welcomed all the children who were brought to him and none were rejected. The last major defence of 'general baptism', R. R. Osborn's *Forbid Them Not*, took its title from the story, and Buchanan is well aware of its dangers.[25] Apologists for indiscriminate baptism have often linked the story with their stress on the universality of God's initiatives and grace. Stacey wrote:

> In receiving all children regardless of the faith of their parents we are repeating what Christ Himself did in His earthly life. The grace of God is for all men, Christ died for all, and all children have, therefore, as their birthright free admittance into the realm of grace. To refuse baptism when it is requested is to attempt to restrict the grace of God.[26]

W. D. Horton from the Reformed tradition wrote similarly:

> To make *anything* the *sine qua non* of baptism is to set a human
> price-tag on what God offers 'gratis' and to erect barriers against
> God's all-embracing love. Conversely, to grant baptism whenever
> it is requested is to respond to God's initiative in coming 'to seek
> and to save the lost', to proclaim the supreme worth of every
> individual in God's sight and to act in harmony with Christ who,
> without screening the parents, welcomed all the children who were
> brought to him.[27]

Baptists have also spotted the implications of the passage.
David Kingdon declared that if infant baptism could be got
out of the passage at all, 'then the text justifies the indiscriminate baptism of all infants, not the restriction of baptism to the
children of believing parents'.[28] David Pawson agreed. 'When
applied to baptism, this passage establishes indiscriminate
baptism.'[29]

With purists wanting more adult baptism and some
Evangelicals wanting less infant baptism, it is no wonder that
Jesus and the children have fared badly. But as with the notion
of adult baptism as the norm, the Church of England is very
much on its own. The story is omitted in the Canadian rite, but
it is one of several authorized gospel readings in the Roman
Catholic rite and in the rites of Australia, Ireland and the
United States. It is a compulsory reading in the Church of
Scotland and in the Methodist Church.

What we miss in every modern rite, though, is Cranmer's
exhortation after the reading which he compiled on the basis of
some words of the Strasbourg reformer, Martin Bucer.[30] Its
expression of warmth and welcome has never been surpassed,
and since the Prayer Book rite is so rarely used today it is worth
printing this exhortation in full:

> Beloved, ye hear in this Gospel the words of our Saviour Christ,
> that he commanded the children to be brought unto him; how
> he blamed those that would have kept them from him; how he
> exhorteth all men to follow their innocency. Ye perceive how by his
> outward gesture and deed he declared his good will toward them;
> for he embraced them in his arms, he laid his hands upon them, and
> blessed them. Doubt ye not therefore, but earnestly believe, that
> he will likewise favourably receive this present infant; that he will

embrace him with the arms of his mercy; that he will give unto him the blessing of eternal life, and make him partaker of his everlasting kingdom. Wherefore we being thus persuaded of the good will of our heavenly Father towards this infant, declared by his Son Jesus Christ; and nothing doubting but that he favourably alloweth this charitable work of ours in bringing this infant to his Holy Baptism; let us faithfully and devoutly give thanks unto him.

Whitaker claimed that parents did not need this 'assurance and encouragement' since it never occurs to them 'to show any modest hesitation, or to doubt whether either the Church or Almighty God might not be willing to receive their children'.[31] He may be right. But if parents do not need this assurance, an increasing number of the clergy certainly need it.

I give the last word here to Bucer:

We ought not only to permit but also to exhort that all children indiscriminately (*promiscue*) be brought to the Lord . . . If there are any goats among them, we can exclude them when they have shown themselves as such. Meanwhile let us not be more scrupulous than Christ, who pronounced children indiscriminately brought to him to be citizens of the kingdom of heaven.[32]

Infant baptism should reflect the welcome which Jesus gave to the children.

NOTES

1. *Infant Baptism Yesterday and Today* (London, Mowbray, 1966), p. 17.
2. W. Barclay, *The Gospel of Matthew* (Edinburgh, St Andrew Press 2nd edn, 1958), ii.233, says strangely that those who brought the children were 'no doubt' their mothers. The suggestion of older brothers and sisters is favoured by Hans-Ruedi Weber, *Jesus and the Children* (Geneva, World Council of Churches, 1979), p. 16.
3. For Jeremias, cf. *Infant Baptism in the First Four Centuries*, pp. 49f.; (b) is mentioned but not commended in Weber, *Jesus and the Children*, p. 18; (c) appears very generally; (d) is the conclusion of the Church of Scotland study document, *The Biblical Doctrine of Baptism* (Edinburgh, St Andrew Press, 1958), p. 48.
4. cf. N. Johansson, 'Making Christians by Sacraments', *Scottish Journal of Theology* V (1952).

5. Jeremias, *Infant Baptism*, pp. 48–53; Aland, *Did the Early Church Baptize Infants?*, pp. 97f.

6. *Baptism in the New Testament* (ET London, SCM, 1950), pp. 71–80.

7. *De Baptismo* 18, ed. E. Evans (London, SPCK, 1964), p. 38.

8. cf. C. E. Pocknee, 'The Gospel Lection in the Rite of Infant Baptism', *Theology* LXII (1959), pp. 496–9; the factual material here is very useful, but the comment needs to be treated with great caution.

9. Text in E. C. Whitaker, *Documents of the Baptismal Liturgy* (London, SPCK, 2nd edn 1970), p. 237.

10. cf. Luther, *Concerning Rebaptism*, ET *Works* (Philadelphia, Fortress, 1955ff), 40:243; Zwingli, *Of Baptism*, ET G. W. Bromiley, *Zwingli and Bullinger* (London, SCM, 1953), p. 153; Bucer, *Strassburg Order of Baptism*, ET J. D. C. Fisher, *Christian Initiation: The Reformation Period* (London, SPCK 1970), p. 38; Calvin, *Institutes* 4:16:7, ET J. T. McNeill and F. L. Battles (London, SCM 1961), 2:1329–31; Bullinger, *Decades* 5:7, ET T. Harding (1849–52), 4:343f.

11. 2:2:31. ET J. Donavan (Dublin *c.* 1829), p. 157.

12. *A Confutation of Unwritten Verities* 10, in *Miscellaneous Writings*, ed. J. E. Cox (Cambridge 1846), p. 60.

13. *Baptism and Confirmation*, p. xv.

14. *The Proposed Services of Baptism and Confirmation Reconsidered*, p. 39.

15. 'The York Revised Service for the Public Baptism of Infants: An Appraisement', *Theology* LXIII (1960), pp. 459–68. Ratcliff was writing not technically to defend the Liturgical Commission's proposals, but to oppose a more conservative rite favoured by the Convocation of York.

16. GS 56, p. 13.

17. *Alternative Services Series 3: Infant Baptism*, GS 225, pp. 5 and 14.

18. *Alternative Services Series 3: Initiation Services*, GS 343.

19. *Initiation Services Series 3*, GS 343X, p. 46.

20. *A Companion to the Alternative Service Book* (London, SPCK, 1986), p. 350.

21. *Knots Untied* (new edn *c.* 1896), p. 121.

22. Motyer, *Baptism in the Book of Common Prayer* (London, Fellowship of Evangelical Churchmen, 1961), pp. 22f.; Hart, op. cit., p. 57; Green, *Baptism* (London, Hodder, 1987), pp. 70–2.

23. *Baptismal Discipline* (Bramcote, 1972), p. 7.

24. *The Liturgy for Infant Baptism (Series 3)* (Bramcote, 1975), p. 13.

25. *A Case for Infant Baptism* (Bramcote, 1973), p. 17.

26. art.cit., p. 188.

27. 'The Pastor's Problems, XII: Baptism for the Asking', *Expository Times* XCIII (1982), p. 296.
28. *Children of Abraham* (1973), p. 86, cited Inchley, *All about Children*, p. 140.
29. *Infant Baptism under Cross-Examination* (Bramcote, 1974), p. 6.
30. Bucer was largely responsible for the section on baptism in Archbishop Hermann of Cologne's *Consultation* published in 1543. ET in J. D. C. Fisher, *Christian Initiation*, pp. 54–69, cf. esp. pp. 59 and 66.
31. *Documents of the Baptismal Liturgy*, p. 40.
32. *Enarrationes in Evangelia Matthaei, Marci et Lucae* (Strasbourg 1527), f. 234r. Bucer repeated this several times, and a translation of a later edition appears in W. Goode, *The Doctrine of the Church of England as to the Effects of Baptism in the Case of Infants* (2nd edn 1850), p. 171.

5

The Faith of the Church

Infant baptism is administered in the faith of the Church

'Baptism', declared a Church of Scotland report, 'depends for its efficacy primarily on the faithfulness of God, and only secondarily on our response of faith.' There may be a danger sometimes of overemphasizing the importance of our own faith. Although in Nazareth Jesus 'could do no mighty work . . . because of their unbelief' (Mark 6.5f.), the Church of Scotland report claims that 'of the individual miracles recorded in the Synoptic Gospels (some twenty-five or thirty) there is reference to faith in only ten or eleven cases'.[1] For most of us this, if true, is startling. But while the Reformers were right to revive the Pauline contrast between faith and good works, faith itself can very subtly become a good work. If it is right to assert that God is not bound by the sacraments, it may also be right to assert that he is not bound by our faith. Certainly he delights to give more than either we desire or deserve.

None the less baptism and faith are closely linked (cf. e.g. Mark 16.16; Acts 8.12, 37f.). In the deepest sense they are inextricably linked, and baptism has long been known as 'the sacrament of faith'. For the Baptist there is no problem here, and baptismal faith is the conscious faith personally confessed by the believing candidate. But although there have been exceptions like Luther, most of those who uphold infant baptism have rejected the idea that infants can bring any kind of personal faith to baptism. They have seen baptismal faith as vicarious faith, the faith of the Church. Ideally of course this includes the faith of the parents, but it has usually been expressed formally not by them but by the godparents, for

41

essentially it is not their faith but the faith of the Church as a whole.

There are abundant examples of vicarious faith in the New Testament, and it is supplied by all sorts of people. In the raising of Jairus' daughter (Mark 5.21–43), and the healing of the Syrophoenician's daughter (Mark 7.24–30), the epileptic (Mark 9.14–29) and the nobleman's son (John 4.46–54) the faith is that of a parent – in three cases the father and only once the mother! But the paralytic benefits from the faith of those who bring him, possibly relations, possibly friends (Mark 2.1–12). The centurion's servant is healed at the request of his master (Matt. 8.5–13). The cripple at the beautiful Gate is cured through the apostles' faith in Jesus (Acts 3.1–16), while the sick in general are saved through the elders' prayer of faith (James 5.13–16).

The concept of vicarious faith is closely related to that of family solidarity, but the New Testament household was larger than the modern family of father, mother and two children, and if household baptisms included children at all, they would have included the children of all the members of the household. Thus if infant baptism first arose as a result of family solidarity, this was already a wider family and a wider solidarity than we normally encounter today. Vicarious faith and an extended family solidarity are both present in the third-century baptismal rite of Hippolytus, 'And they shall baptize the little children first. And if they can answer for themselves, let them answer. But if they cannot, let their parents answer or someone from their family'.[2]

But both concepts involved problems, and *c*.408 St Augustine was asked by his friend Boniface whether parental idolatry harmed children and, if not, how parental faith could help them. In his reply he made three points of continuing importance. First, it was the Spirit who both made regeneration possible through the agency of another's will and who actually regenerated. John 3.5 spoke of rebirth not 'by the will of the child's parents, or by the faith of those presenting him, or of those administering the ordinance' but 'by water and the Spirit'. Secondly, he urged (and he might have been writing today):

> Do not be troubled by the fact that some bring their little ones for baptism not in the believing expectation of their being born again to eternal life by spiritual grace but because they think it is a medicine for recovering or retaining physical health.

Provided that the necessary actions were performed and the necessary sacramental words pronounced, the new birth was not impeded, for sometimes the Spirit worked not merely through the ignorant but also through the downright unworthy. In any case, and this was his third point, infants were offered 'not so much by those in whose arms they are carried (although they are offered in part by them if they are good believers) as by the whole company of saints and believers . . . by whose holy and indivisible charity they are helped to share in the communion of the Holy Spirit.' Mother Church was the true parent, and there were many like slaves, orphans and foundlings who could not be presented for baptism by their natural parents and had to be presented instead 'by those who have the opportunity of this work of mercy'.[3]

Augustine was not infallible, and we have rejected his link between baptism and original guilt as based on a mistranslation of St Paul and constituting a deviation from the tradition. But here he was faithful to the tradition, and in a manner wholly consonant with Scripture he developed the earlier concept of family solidarity into the richer concept of 'a solidarity of mankind in grace . . . parallel to the solidarity of the human race in sin'.[4] This understanding now became general, and the scholastics were content to repeat it without any attempt to improve on it.[5]

In Augustine's time it was still customary for parents to act as sponsors for their children although, as the passage quoted makes clear, this was not invariably the case. But Pseudo-Dionysius writing a century or so later described it as a condition of infant baptism that parents should transfer the charge of their children to a godfather (*theiō patri*) who was clearly distinct from the child's natural father,[6] and soon the theory developed that the spiritual relationship of sponsorship was incompatible with the natural relationship of parenthood. Sponsorship involved both presenting the child at the font and receiving or raising him from the font, with the implication of future spiritual responsibility for him, and according to the new theory 'One who had "received" or "raised" an infant, born in a state of sin, could not "receive" or "raise" that infant from the font, regenerated and washed clean'.[7] In 813 the Council of Mainz decreed that 'no one may raise his own son or daughter from the baptismal font',[8] and in the thirteenth century St Thomas Aquinas wrote, 'As spiritual and natural birth differ, so there ought also to be a different education . . . Therefore the spiritual father ought to be someone other than the earthly father, unless there is some necessity for the contrary'.[9] In England, the *Sarum Manual* decreed that 'the father or the mother must not raise their own child from the sacred font . . . save in constraint of extreme necessity', and throughout the rite it was the godparents who were addressed and who gave the answers. The parents were mentioned only in one peripheral rubric, 'Let the father and mother be enjoined to preserve their child from fire and water and all other dangers until the age of seven years'.[10] Apart from this, the rite did not even imply their presence.

From one point of view this minimizing of the role of parents was extremely unfortunate, though Mark Searle has charitably suggested that 'perhaps in medieval society the extended family played a larger role than it does today, so that the faith and practice of the parents were less crucial'.[11] But from another point of view it made it abundantly clear that the infant's right to baptism lay not essentially in the faith of its parents but, as Augustine had explained, in the faith of the Church of which the sponsors were the spokesmen.

At the Reformation, Luther abandoned the ideas of vicarious faith and the faith of the Church in favour of his own theory (a strange one to us) that infants had a personal faith of their own.[12] Zwingli on the other hand argued that the demand for faith did not apply to infants,[13] and he laid the foundation of a new rationale for their baptism. This rationale involved four assertions: first, that Abraham's faith was reckoned to him as righteousness (Gen. 15.6); second, that God entered into a covenant with Abraham and his seed on the basis of this faith (Gen. 17.10); third, that the sign and seal of this covenant was circumcision; fourth, that its sign and seal now is baptism.[14] The crucial points here are that the covenant is based on faith, that it is made not only with the man of faith but also with his seed, and that baptism is its sign and seal. On this understanding the children of believers are born 'within' the covenant. They are 'holy', and they are baptized not in order that their status before God may somehow be changed but as a sign and seal of their existing status.

Zwingli never worked out this position in any detail, but Bucer took it further and in his 1525–30 Strasbourg rite he described baptism, like circumcision, as an initiatory sign testifying 'that the infant must be of God's people (until he shows himself otherwise by a wicked life afterwards) because he is born of Christian parents'.[15] But Bucer was more prolific than systematic, and it was left to Calvin to perfect this covenant theology and to relate it more definitively to baptism. Essentially,

> The children of believers are baptised not in order that they who were previously strangers to the church may then for the first time become children of God, but rather that, because by the blessing of the promise they already belonged to the body of Christ, they are received into the church with this solemn sign.

If with Abraham the sacrament followed faith, with Isaac it preceded it. Thus 'infants are baptised into future repentance and faith, and even though these have not yet been formed in them, the seed of both lies hidden within them by the secret working of the Spirit.'[16]

In itself, and in its understanding of the meaning and effects of baptism, this particular brand of covenant theology represented a radical break with the past, but for our purposes the difference was not as large as it might seem. In one sense it merely substituted 'the faith of the covenant people' for 'the faith of the Church', and the covenant people *were* the Church. Nonetheless, though, since the covenant promise was passed on through the parents, the parents now acquired a new importance. Calvin's 1542 rite assumes at least the father's presence,[17] and in Bucer's 1543 rite in Hermann's *Consultation*

45

both parents are normally present and join with the godparents in making the baptismal renunciations and professions of faith in their own names as well as in the name of the child.[18] But the important thing for us is that neither Bucer nor Calvin restricted baptism to the children of faithful parents. God had made his covenant with Abraham and his seed, but 'seed' seems to have been understood in a broad sense since the covenant sign of circumcision was enjoined on 'every male throughout your generations, whether born in your house, or bought with your money' (Gen. 17.12). Bucer interpreted 'seed' in an equally broad sense, and he urged that infants should be baptized whether born of Christian parents or simply under the authority of Christians. Even the infants of the ungodly 'since they are born more to the community than to their natural parents, should be initiated by Christ's sacrament when they are dedicated by the Church to Christ, for they have been consecrated by the Lord, their greater parent'. In these circumstances, the ungodly parents were to 'desire their kinsfolk or other friends which be as yet the true and lively members of the church that in their stead they will ask baptism for their infants'. At one point Bucer went even further than the medievals, and gave the civil authorities the right to baptize compulsorily children whose parents refused to have them baptized.[19]

Calvin had no doubt that baptism was profaned if administered without regular churchmembers as sponsors, but he emphasized that God's promise not only comprehended the offspring of the faithful in the first degree but was extended to a thousand generations. The progeny of pious ancestors belonged to the body of the Church even when their grandfathers and parents were apostates, and 'wherever the profession of Christianity has not wholly perished or become extinct, infants are defrauded of their right if they are kept from the common symbol'.[20] Bullinger, Zwingli's successor in Zurich, expressed himself in an even more traditional way: 'But the father doth not believe. Be it so; yet that is no hindrance to the infant; for in the faith of the church he is brought to be baptised.'[21]

46

In England the Reformation proceeded at a slower pace, and comparatively little attention was given to baptism in the early stages. The 1549 Prayer Book was remarkably conservative. It bore no traces at all of covenant theology, and the only part played by the parents is to give advance notice (of less than 24 hours) to the curate that baptism is desired. They play no part whatever in the service itself, and even their presence is not assumed. As in the medieval rite, it is the godparents who bring the children, who respond for them and who are charged with their spiritual care. In 1552 the rite was revised in a more Protestant direction and shorn of some of its ceremonies, but there were no changes at all at these points.

In the last century William Goode, the foremost Evangelical writer on baptism, declared that 'Children are baptised in our Church as the children of believers, as our early divines constantly affirm; and therefore all statements on the subject of their baptism must be interpreted on that *supposition*.'[22] If by believers Goode meant simply baptized people who professed at least a nominal Christianity – as opposed to the Jews, Turks and Infidels of the Good Friday collect – this is of course true, even a truism. But if he meant believers in the stronger sense which the Reformers themselves attached to the word, the statement is wholly misleading. There is not a word to justify it in either of Edward VI's Prayer Books, and very few words in 'our early divines'.

During Queen Mary's reign, however, many English Protestants took refuge on the continent and saw for themselves the doctrine and discipline of the reformed Churches. These Churches were now wrestling with some of the questions implicit in the new theology but not always clearly discerned at first. One was godparents: could there, in normal circumstances, be any justification for excluding the parents from this role? Another was ungodliness. Not all the children of Christian parents, as they grew up, showed themselves to be godly. Their holiness might be presumed when they were infants, but could it be presumed any longer if their adult life seemed to deny it? And if they themselves spurned the covenant and were unfaithful, how could their children be deemed holy and thus eligible for baptism? Perhaps Bucer and Calvin had been too liberal here.

On Mary's death the exiles returned to England anxious to see further reformation. But no change was made to baptismal procedures in the 1559 Prayer Book, and in 1561 a Royal Order had to decree 'That neither the curates nor the parents of the children alter the common used manner for godfathers and godmothers to answer for the children'.[23] Despite this, in the 1562/63 Convocation sixty-four clergy requested that the father be present if possible and that along with the godparents he should openly profess the faith and express the desire that the infant be baptized in that faith.[24] But Archbishop Parker would have none of this, and in his 1566 *Advertisements* he ordered curates to baptize 'without charging the parent to be present or absent at the christening of his child, although the parent may be present, or absent, but not to answer as godfather for his child'.[25]

In retrospect the official attitude may seem unduly harsh here. But Parker knew that moderate demands would quickly lead to more rigid demands. He was happy for parents to be present at their child's baptism. But once it was permissible for them to make the responses there would soon be the demand that they should be compelled to make the responses, and this would have involved the Church of England in a completely new restriction of baptism to the children of the godly. Harsh he may have been, but he was wiser in his generation than we have been in ours.

In 1572 the Puritans launched a full-scale attack on the Prayer Book with *An Admonition to the Parliament*. Their position was now clear: 'The children of the faithful only are to be baptised', and it was the father's duty to make 'an open confession of that faith, wherein he would have his child baptised'.[26] But John Whitgift, later Archbishop of Canterbury, was wholly dismissive of this. 'What scripture have you', he asked, 'that the parent at the baptizing of his child should make a rehearsal of his faith?', and

> What if the parents be of evil behaviour? what if it be the child of a drunkard or of an harlot? what if the parents be papists? what if

they be heretics? . . . shall not their children be baptised? . . . I fear few do perceive the poison that lieth hid under these words. May not a wicked father have a good child? may not a papist or heretic have a believing son? will you seclude for the parent's sake (himself being baptised) his seed from baptism?

If the *Admonition* did not 'comprehend those under the name of faithful which be baptized . . . it passeth man's understanding to know who be faithful indeed'.[27]

Thomas Cartwright, replying for the Puritans, objected that Whitgift

doth make of the holy sacrament of baptism (which is an entry into the house of God, and whereby only the family of God must enter) a common passage whereby he will have clean and unclean, holy and profane, as well those that are without the covenant, as those that be within it, to pass by; and so maketh the church no household, but an inn to receive whosoever cometh.

Whitgift answered that he made the sacrament 'no other kind of "passage" than God himself hath made it' and the church had ever used it. None could tell who was clean or unclean, holy or profane, and all must needs pass by it. As for the children of the ungodly, 'can any fault of the parents, having once received the seal of the covenant, seclude their children from receiving the same seal?'.[28]

Richard Hooker was equally firm:

A wrong conceit that none may receive the sacrament of baptism but they whose parents at the least the one of them are by the soundness of their religion and by their virtuous demeanour known to be men of God, hath caused some to repel children whosoever bring them if their parents be mispersuaded in religion, or for other misdeserts excommunicated; some likewise for that cause to withhold baptism, unless the father, albeit no such exception can justly be taken against him, do notwithstanding make profession of his faith, and avouch the child to be his own. Thus whereas God hath appointed them ministers of holy things, they make themselves inquisitors of men's persons a great deal farther than need is.

Such people should consider that God had ordained baptism 'in favour of mankind'. To restrict favours was an odious thing, but to enlarge them was acceptable both to God and man. In any case, it was the Church which through the ministry of those who presented them offered children to baptism, and it was 'against both duty and equity to refuse the mother of believers herself, and not to take her in this case for a faithful parent'.[29]

The Prayer Book position was strongly reaffirmed in the new canons issued in 1604. Canon 29, *Fathers not to be Godfathers in baptism, and Children not Communicants not to be Godparents in baptism*, read: 'No parent shall be urged to be present, nor be admitted to answer as Godfather for his own Child . . . neither shall any person be admitted Godfather or Godmother to any Child at Christening or Confirmation, before the said person so undertaking hath received the holy communion.' Canon 68, *Ministers not to refuse to Christen or Bury*, ordered that no minister 'shall refuse or delay to christen any child . . . that is brought to the Church to him upon Sundays or Holy-days to be christened', and thus firmly rejected the Puritan distinction between the children of the godly and those of the ungodly. Canon 69 forbade ministers to defer christenings at home if an infant was in danger of death.[30]

At the Savoy Conference held in 1661 'to advise upon and review' the Prayer Book, the Puritans presented a list of *Exceptions*. They objected first that many pious ministers judged it unlawful to baptize children 'whose parents both of them are atheists, infidels, heretics, or unbaptised . . . excommunicate persons, fornicators, or otherwise notorious and scandalous sinners', and they desired that they might not be compelled to baptize the children of such 'until they have made due profession of their repentance'. But the bishops deemed this desire 'very hard and uncharitable, punishing the poor infants for the parents' sakes, and giving also too great and arbitrary power to the minister'. They added that 'our church concludes more charitably, that Christ will favourably accept every infant to baptism, that is presented by the church according to our present order', and that this conclusion was both scriptural and catholic.

The Puritans next objected that when mention was made of

the godparents there was no mention of the parents 'in whose right the child is baptised, and who are fittest both to dedicate it unto God, and to covenant for it'. Only the parents, or others appointed by them, had power to consent for the children or to enter them into covenant, and it should be left free to parents 'whether they will have sureties to undertake for their children in baptism or no'. But the bishops thought it 'an erroneous doctrine, and the ground of many others . . . that children have no other right to baptism than in their parents' right'. Primitive practice forbade it to be left to parents whether or not there should be other sureties, and it was fit that 'the practice of venerable antiquity' should be carefully observed.

The Puritans also requested that in the Catechism 'the entering infants into God's covenant may be more warily expressed' since it is 'to the seed of believers that the covenant of God is made; and not (that we can find) to all that have such believing sureties, who are neither parents nor pro-parents of the child'. The bishops replied here that the effect of children's baptism did not depend 'upon the faith and repentance of their natural parents or pro-parents, or of their godfathers or godmothers; but upon the ordinance and institution of Christ'.[31]

As the Puritan demands make clear, many people at this time did believe that the covenant-faith of parents was the ground of infant baptism. But the revisers of the Prayer Book firmly rejected this view. 1662 made no significant changes here, and still the only part played by parents was the preliminary notifying to the curate. By canon law they were explicitly forbidden to act as godparents, and even their presence was not required. The godparents, who by canon law must be communicants, acted not in their own right but as the ministerial agents of the Church, and it was the faith of the Church vicariously offered which made baptism possible. It was on this ground that the Prayer Book in no way restricted baptism to the children of faithful parents. If the parents were faithful, their children were richly blessed. If they were not, their children should not be further deprived.

All this was splendidly expressed two centuries later by

51

Bishop George Moberly of Salisbury in his 1868 Bampton Lectures:

> That which the mother brings is, first, faith. The infant, incapable by age of coming in faith of his own, comes in borrowed faith. But from whom is his faith borrowed? Is it from his natural parents? Yes, no doubt, in part, if they be good and faithful. But what if they be evil and unfaithful? Is it from his sponsors? Yes, again, if they be good and faithful. But no man can say for certain that they are so; and God forbid that the spiritual life of the poor child should be thought to be dependent on so frail and uncertain a support as their faith! Nay, it is upon the faith of the Church of Christ, whom the sponsors on the special occasion and for the special purpose represent.[32]

Infant baptism is administered in the faith of the Church.

NOTES

1. *The Biblical Doctrine of Baptism*, pp. 56–60.
2. *Apostolic Tradition* 21.3, ed. G. Dix (London, SPCK, 1968), p. 33.
3. *Ep.* 98.1–6 (CSEL 34.520–8). ETs in *Letters*, ed. M. Dods (Edinburgh, 1875), 2.14–20; and A. Hamman, *Baptism: Ancient Liturgies and Patristic Texts* (New York, 1967), pp. 221–6.
4. E. R. Fairweather, 'St Augustine's Interpretation of Infant Baptism', *Augustinus Magister* (Paris, 1954f.), 2.897–903.
5. cf. St Thomas Aquinas, *Summa Theologiae* 3.68–9, ET J. J. Cunningham (1975), 57.106–11.
6. *De Ecclesiastica Hierarchia* 7.3–11 (PG 3.568).
7. D. S. Bailey, *Sponsors at Baptism and Confirmation* (London, SPCK, 1952), p. 81.
8. *ibid.*, p. 83.
9. *Summa Theologiae* 3.67–8, ET 57.79.
10. Whitaker, *Documents of the Baptismal Liturgy*, p. 248.
11. *Christening: The Making of Christians* (Collegeville, MN, Liturgical Press, 1980), p. 28.
12. cf. e.g. ibid., 40.241–6.
13. *Of baptism*, ET G. W. Bromiley, *Zwingli and Bullinger*, pp. 139–46.
14. ibid., p. 138.
15. ET J. D. C. Fisher, *Christian Initiation*, p. 35.
16. *Institutes* 4.15–22; 4.16–24; 4.16–20; ed.cit. 2.1323; 1346f.; 1343.

17. ET J. D. C. Fisher, *Christian Initiation*, pp. 112–17.
18. ibid., pp. 54–69.
19. *Metaphrasis et Enarratio in Ep. ad Romanos* (Basle, 1562), pp. 161, 331; *Consultation*, ET J. D. C. Fisher, *Christian Initiation*, p. 56; cf. also W. P. Stephens, *The Holy Spirit in the Theology of Martin Bucer* (Cambridge University Press 1970), p. 234.
20. *Ep.* 3128, to John Knox (CR 45.665–68).
21. *Decades* 5.7, ed.cit., 4.344.
22. *The Doctrine of the Church of England as to the Effects of Baptism in the Case of Infants*, p. 14.
23. no. 7, W. H. Frere and W. M. Kennedy, *Visitation Articles and Injunctions* (1910), iii.110.
24. J. Strype, *Annals of the Reformation* (Oxford, 1824), 1.1.508.
25. no. lxxxi, in H. Gee and W. J. Hardy, *Documents Illustrative of English Church History* (1896), p. 471.
26. *Puritan Manifestos*, ed. W. H. Frere and C. E. Douglas (London, SPCK, 1954), pp. 14f., 27.
27. *Works*, ed. J. Ayre (Cambridge 1851–3), iii.134–8.
28. ibid., iii.139–45.
29. *Laws of Ecclesiastical Polity*, 5.64–5, ed. J. Keble (Oxford, 1850), ii.50f.
30. *Constitutions and Canons Ecclesiastical* (1604) (London, SPCK, 1960), pp. 11f., 29f.
31. E. Cardwell, *History of Conferences* (Oxford, 1849), pp. 323–7 and 355–8.
32. *The Administration of the Holy Spirit in the Body of Christ* (1883), pp. 146f.

6

The Faith of the Child

Infant baptism looks forward to the child's growth as a Christian

'Baptism, of itself', declared the Second Vatican Council, 'is only a beginning, a point of departure, for it is wholly directed toward the acquiring of fullness of life in Christ.'[1] The Church has always been concerned not only with baptism itself but with what it implies and what should follow from it, and four things have traditionally been stressed here.

First of all, from the moment of an infant's baptism, the faith of the Church is his faith. Liturgies are conservative things, and the baptismal liturgy which developed when most candidates were adults was slow to adapt itself to infants. The responses made by (sponsors for) infants were the same as those made by adults for themselves, and there was an important point here: it was the child, not the parents or sponsors, who was being baptized. But by modern thinking there is an air of unreality about treating an infant as responsible if inarticulate, and our own doubts were felt much earlier. Augustine's correspondent, Boniface, pointed out that no one could foretell an infant's behaviour or guess his present thoughts (if any), and asked how therefore his parents could answer for him. If asked whether he would grow up chaste and honest, they would hesitate; 'Yet when asked, "Does he believe in God" – when he does not even know if there is a God – they reply unhesitatingly, "he believes".' Augustine replied that the sacred rites took their names from the mysteries they represented, and so 'in a certain manner' we receive faith through the sacrament of faith.[2] In other words, the infant becomes a believer through being joined by the sacrament of faith to the household of faith. The medievals took this further, and St Thomas spoke of an infusion of faith at baptism – not actual faith, which required the activity of the will which children did not have, but habitual faith, which required only the will itself which children did have.[3] This of course is speculative, but there are some people who can confirm Augustine's more general language from their own experience. They speak of never having known what it is not to believe. Belief was part of the air they breathed in their infancy, and it was something of their own from their earliest recollection.

Secondly, from the moment of his baptism the infant is 'bound' by the renunciations and professions made on his behalf, 'bound' by the faith of the Church as his own baptismal faith. The idea of baptism as not just a present profession but a binding pledge may even be explicit in the New Testament (if *eperōtēma* in 1 Peter 3.21 is translated as 'pledge' rather than 'appeal'), but it was certainly implicit in the New Testament and was frequently emphasized by the Fathers.[4] St Thomas spoke of an infant as 'obligated' to the faith of the Church,[5] and at the Reformation Erasmus got himself into trouble for suggesting that infants be asked to renew their baptismal profession, on pain of suspension from the sacraments if they refused. It was an innocent enough suggestion, but the objection was to their being 'asked' to renew it. They were *already* bound by it, and they had no choice but to honour it![6] A similar view is adopted in the Prayer Book Catechism. The child rehearses the three things which his godparents promised and vowed in his name. The catechist then asks, 'Dost thou not think that thou art bound to believe, and to do as they have promised for thee?', and the child answers, 'Yes verily', and heartily thanks God for calling him to this state of salvation.

Thirdly, the infant's baptism in the faith of the Church looks forward to his growth in that faith. Augustine admitted that the infant believer did not yet have that faith which included the consent of the will, but said that he would understand the meaning of the sacrament when he grew up, and with the consent of the will would then conform himself to its truth.[7] This was of course an idealized picture, but the hope or even the expectation of such consenting faith was a natural one. Although in most rites the sponsors continued to affirm in the name of the child, 'I believe', there were occasional variations: in the eighth-century Bobbio Missal the sponsors replied, 'Let him believe', or 'Let us hope he will believe',[8] and in some manuscripts of the eleventh-century Spanish *Liber Ordinum* they reply, 'He shall believe'.[9] Even where the traditional words were used, there was an increasing tendency to interpret them in a future sense. Peter Lombard said that 'the promise is made for the child, that if he grows up he will renounce the devil and keep the faith'.[10] Robert Paululus said that it was made 'with regard to his behaviour if he comes to years of discretion',[11] and Alan of Lille described it as a pledge of 'the faith which he will have at the appointed time'.[12] In the Prayer Book the godparents still declare 'in the name of this child' 'I renounce' and 'I steadfastly believe', but this is explained as a promise that he 'will' renounce and believe. After the baptism prayer is offered that he 'may lead the rest of his life according to this beginning'. The Prayer Book also contains, apart from the baptismal charge to the godparents, a rubric that 'all Fathers, Mothers, Masters, and Dames, shall cause their Children, Servants, and Prentices' to attend church on Sundays and holydays to be instructed and examined in the Catechism.

Fourthly, those who sponsor the child for baptism and profess the faith on his behalf are also sureties for his growth in the faith. It was because this was such a perilous undertaking for the sponsors that Tertullian advocated the deferment of baptism,[13] and as Boniface pointed out no one could really be sure how a child would develop. But just as the sponsors of adults were to be vigilant in 'advising, counselling and correcting',[14] so too the sponsors of an infant, by making the professions on his behalf, were promising godly instruction that would persuade the child to honour these professions.[15] St Thomas accepted that where children are 'raised among Catholic Christians, sponsors can be excused from their concern, presuming that the children are diligently instructed

by the parents'.[16] Similarly in the *Sarum Manual* the godparents, who are described as 'sureties before God', are
charged to 'learn or see it be learned the Our Father, Hail
Mary, and I believe . . . and in all goodly haste to be
confirmed'.[17] The godparents are not meant to be officious,
but if they do not give the instruction themselves they are to
make sure that somebody else does. Theirs is the ultimate
responsibility. The Prayer Book, however, is stricter. There is
no mention of anyone else at this point, and it is the godparents
who are charged, 'Forasmuch as this child hath promised by
you his sureties . . . ye must remember that it is your parts and
duties to see that this Infant be taught, so soon as he shall be
able to learn, what a solemn vow, promise and profession he
hath here made by you.' In particular they are to provide that
he hear sermons; learn the Creed, Lord's Prayer, Ten
Commandments and all other things which he ought to know
and believe; be brought up to lead a godly and Christian life;
and be brought to the Bishop to be confirmed as soon as he has
been duly instructed.

As we saw in the last chapter, the Prayer Book upheld the
faith of the Church as the theological basis of infant baptism
and the 1662 revisers repelled the attack of the 'covenant'
school. But the next challenge to the Prayer Book pattern was a
more practical one, and it arose from the widespread break-
down of the system of sponsors and sureties. With the rise of
the industrial revolution, society became more mobile and, cut
off from their families in the large new urban parishes and
often with only tenuous links with the Church, many parents
found it increasingly difficult to find godparents. Sometimes
recourse was had to semi-professional godparents, and sometimes there were no godparents at all. Urban clergy, eager to
counter the growing neglect of baptism, were thankful to see
any godparents, and the canon requiring that godparents be
communicants was largely ignored.[18] An attempt was now
made to remove the prohibition on parents acting as godparents, and this would have meant that only one non-parental
godparent was required. A canon removing the prohibition
was actually published by the Convocation of Canterbury in

1865, but it failed to receive Royal Letters Patent confirming it and it never came into effect.[19]

The lack of godparents, and especially of suitable ones, might not have mattered too much in small parishes where the conscientious pastor could still know his flock personally or in areas where the general mood of the populace exercised a Christian influence. It might not have mattered too much again in parishes where baptisms were fairly few in number and could still be administered (as the Prayer Book so clearly envisaged) in the course of Sunday worship and with the prayerful support of the congregation. But none of these things applied in the large urban parishes, and in 1896, less than thirty years after Moberly had so movingly described the theological understanding of baptism, Hensley Henson from his experience of Barking painted a very different picture of its actual administration:

> On a weekday evening, or on Sunday afternoons, times when the absence of the congregation can be counted upon, the priest in a large town parish takes his stand at the font to administer the Sacrament of Holy Baptism to all who desire it. The candidates arrive in the arms of their mothers, who are sometimes assisted on these occasions by the monthly nurse, or a neighbour to whom baptisms and burials have an attraction not possessed by the other ordinances of religion, or by a district visitor, or even, though this is almost unknown, by the father. No inquiries of any kind are addressed to them beyond the questions as to names and addresses necessary for the filling in of the register. The service proceeds; there are no sponsors save those whom I have mentioned. Often they cannot read; oftener they won't. They do not answer the questions, so solemn and important, which are addressed to the sponsors; but with persistence the priest may, if he deem it worth his while, succeed in getting them to say after him the required responses. The service is over in half an hour, and the party retires to the pothouse and the slum.

It was in this context that Henson made his protest against 'the modern practice of unconditioned, indiscriminate baptizing'. He argued that the Church had always exacted securities for the Christian upbringing of the infants she baptized, and that without such securities infant baptism could not be justified. But in the circumstances of urban life the traditional securities were proving worthless, and neither home, day school, Sunday school nor even church itself were providing adequate alternatives. Reform was essential, 'immediate and thorough, though cautious and gradual'. Canvassing for baptisms should be stopped, and the Church should face 'the necessity of greatly reducing the number of the baptized'. The requirement of communicant godparents should be enforced 'wherever reasonably practical', and parishes should consider forming guilds of sponsors, all communicants, whose members would stand as sponsors where necessary and who would combine 'for mutual counsel and intercession'.[20]

Darwell Stone, the Anglo-Catholic leader, writing at the same time as Henson, stressed that 'it might matter less who the sponsors, regarded as representatives of the universal Church, individually are, if the Church herself . . . could securely provide for the Christian training of the baptized'. Sudden or violent action by bishops or clergy on the selection of sponsors, 'coming after long tolerated and widely prevalent laxity', might prove harmful, and what was needed was 'clear and persistent teaching of the doctrine of Baptism and the meaning of sponsorship'.[21] But not all were as patient as Stone, and in 1907 Roland Allen, a former missionary in China, resigned his living at Chalfont St Peter in rural Buckinghamshire in protest at the situation. It had become customary, he complained, for people who made no profession of believing the Church's doctrines or keeping the Church's laws to demand her offices as if they were theirs by natural inheritance.

In consequence we see the strange and painful sight of men and women who habitually neglect their religious duties, or who openly deny the truth of the Creeds, or who by the immorality of their lives openly defy the laws of God, standing up as sponsors in a Christian church, before a Christian minister, in the presence of a Christian congregation and as representatives of the Church on behalf of a new-born child solemnly professing their desire for Holy Baptism, their determination to renounce the world, the flesh and the devil, their steadfast faith in the Creed and their willingness to obey God's holy will, whilst they know, and everyone in the church knows, that they themselves neither do, nor intend to do, any of these things. Then they are solemnly directed to see that the child is taught the faith and practice which they set at naught.

He realized that he was not legally bound to admit any but communicants as sponsors, but custom 'more powerful often than law' compelled his acquiescence in a practice he could not justify.[22]

The 1928 Prayer Book, had it been authorized, would have allowed two godparents in cases where three could not 'conveniently be had', and it also provided 'if need so require' that parents themselves might be sponsors provided that the child still had one other sponsor – though 'if need so require' suggested that parental godparents were rather a second best. But the situation was still not improving, and in 1939 a Convocation report recognized that (as in Henson's day)

the requisite number of godparents is not always insisted upon, and it is not usual for the officiating priest to take any steps to enquire as to the suitability of such sponsors as are forthcoming. The association of the baptized infant with the Church very commonly terminates at baptism, since the sponsors are often entirely indifferent to their pledges.

Convocation agreed that the clergyman's duty of admonishing people not to defer their children's baptism included 'the responsibility of urging and assisting the parents to secure suitable godparents and to undertake that the child should be brought up in the Christian faith and life'. They recommended that at least a week's notice be given before baptism, and that clergy should visit the home as soon as possible to explain the meaning of the service and the duties of the godparents. They should enquire about the spiritual fitness of the proposed godparents, bearing in mind the ideal of communicant god- parents, and they might also point out (an advance on 1928) that 'parents may often be the best godparents'. Convocation also recommended that a sponsors' guild 'might supply godparents to represent the congregation . . . into which the baptized child is received', and that contact should be maintained with the family after the baptism.[23]

It was also in 1939 that a group of clergy from Poplar issued a report, and this went much further than the Convocation report. They were unable to make any adequate suggestions about godparents since the difficulty of providing communicant godparents was enormous. But in any case, even when there were communicant godparents it was the parents who actually influenced the child. They therefore concentrated their suggestions on the parents, and recommended instruction classes of four, eight or even twelve weeks. They also recommended that baptism should always be refused where there was strong reason to believe that the child would not be brought up as a Christian; failure to send older children to church or for confirmation would provide such reason.[24] In 1940 A. R. Vidler supported the Poplar clergy in an impassioned editorial in *Theology* entitled 'Baptismal Disgrace'. The Convocation report he described as 'meagre and miserable'. There would be no lead from the bishops, and we must look instead to the junior clergy to rise up in revolt.[25]

The battle-lines were now being drawn up, and three more official reports followed: *Confirmation Today* in 1944, *Baptism Today* in 1949 and *Baptism and Confirmation Today* in 1955. But before *Baptism Today* was published, there were discussions at the 1948 Lambeth Conference. The Conference reaffirmed that infant baptism presupposed that the infant would be brought up in the faith and practice of the Church, reminded parents that they had a major share in the responsibility for this, and urged the clergy to put them in mind of this duty. It recommended that all godparents should be baptized, that at least one should be a practising Anglican communicant, that churchpeople should be encouraged to offer themselves as sponsors, 'whether as members of a Sponsors' Guild or in some other way', and that parents should be permitted to act as godparents if otherwise eligible. It also called the attention of godparents to the seriousness of their promises and recommended to the clergy the system of the 'Baptismal Roll'.[26]

Baptism Today endorsed most of these proposals, but it could not go much further since there were now three groups in the Church: those who would not refuse or delay baptism in any circumstances, those who would administer it only when there was assurance of a Christian upbringing and those who for the present sought improvements in practice rather than radical reform. It did, however, suggest some questions for discussion by the clergy.[27] The replies, as summarized in the 1955 report, revealed that most clergy regarded infant baptism as a pastoral opportunity for evangelism, and that on theological, practical and pastoral grounds 'the overwhelming majority' were against the deferment of baptism. But there was little support for the stiffening of discipline with regard to godparents, and little enthusiasm for, or experience of, Sponsor's Guilds. For its own part, *Baptism and Confirmation Today* recommended that the importance of choosing suitable godparents should be emphasized when notice of baptism was given; that as far as possible the minister should see the parents and godparents before the service to explain their responsibilities to them; and that even when baptism was not administered at Morning or Evening Prayer 'a congregation representing the Church should be encouraged to attend'.[28]

The debate now ceased for a while, and the conclusions at this stage were reflected in the Liturgical Commission's 1958 report and its proposed new service. This formally assumed the presence of the parents, and coupled them with the sponsors in an opening address, similar to the Prayer Book's concluding one, on the duty of providing a Christian upbringing. But it did not ask the parents to make the renunciations or the professions, and it was still the sponsors who had brought the children who were asked to 'make on their behalf the promises, which they will renew in their own persons, when they are brought in due time to be confirmed'.[29] The balance here was excellent. Parents were reminded of their duties, but it was still the godparents who formally sponsored the children and accepted responsibility for their Christian upbringing.

The criticisms of the previous century had demonstrated that the sponsorial system was not always working well in practice, but they had failed to establish that the system itself was wrong. The right kind of godparents can still play a vital role in the nurturing of the children's faith. The Methodist

Church, which in the past placed all the emphasis on the parents, now formally provides for optional sponsors to assist the parents: 'one chosen by the parents, and the other, who shall normally be a member of the church in which the Baptism takes place, by the Minister'. The Orthodox writer Alexander Schmemann claims that godparents are 'more needed than ever', and again suggests that one of them be appointed not by the family but by the parish priest, and be charged with following up the child and reporting problems to the priest: 'The essential point in all this is that sponsorship is an important spiritual function within the Church and that therefore the Church, and not the family, ought to define and control it.'[30] This is easier said than done. But we must not forget Moberly's statement that the godparents 'on the special occasion and for the special purpose' represent the universal Church. Every effort should be made to influence parents' choice in the right direction, and in many areas there is little excuse for not insisting that two at least be confirmed.

Godparents are 'an outward and visible sign' of the universal Church. They are the Church's spokesmen during the baptism service and the Church's agents after it. The Doctrine Commission of the Church in Wales has argued that 'personalizing the vicarious responsibility of the whole people of God in the activity of particular individuals, not only reminds the congregation of its own function, but also secures that this function be discharged'.[31] Ideally this is true, but if the godparents cannot or will not fulfil their responsibilities, the Church's responsibility remains. The role of the godparents as individuals must not be exaggerated in the name of 'the faith of the Church' any more than the role of the parents should be exaggerated in the name of covenant theology. As the present Archbishop of York has said,

> I . . . want to see Baptism primarily expressing the faith of the Church, and the kind of commitment which is made there is the commitment of the Church and not necessarily that of the parents and godparents; and in expressing this faith the Church then expresses God's claim upon this individual life.[32]

The sponsorial system saves us from an undue concentration on parental faith and focuses the attention where it belongs, on the faith of the Church. In baptizing in this faith, the Church herself accepts the ultimate responsibility for spiritual nurture. She also expresses a belief, as far as England is concerned, that under God her faith, her presence in all parts of the country and the continuing Christian influences in society are such that there is still the real possibility that the child will have some kind of Christian upbringing. As Moss pointed out, attitudes to baptism are often related to assessments of society, but even the most pessimistic judge of our society would admit that there are possibilities here which would not be present if a clergyman on holiday in Tibet were to baptize 'indiscriminately' all the infants he saw there, and then return home.

Because of the Church's weakness today, our success in nurturing the baptized is small, and we have to speak more of possibilities of Christian nurture than of guarantees or assurances. But even the guarantee of Christian nurture can never be a guarantee of active Christian faith. Not all the children of active Christian parents grow up to be active Christian believers themselves, and even those baptized as adults do not always remain faithful. There are problems here whatever position we adopt, but those attaching to the open view are no greater than those attaching to other views. Kuhrt claims that 'the policy of general baptism has had a long innings but has clearly not stemmed the rising tide of secularism and unbelief'.[33] In part this is true. But greater rigour has also failed to stem it. From 1900 to 1950 the Church of England consistently baptized 64%–70% of the infant population. Since then there has been a steady decline to our present 32%, and no one can claim that the Church or the country is the better for this. The increasing secularization of society and the growth in the adherents of other religions have both played a part in the decline, but so too has the increasing rigour of many clergy. If we baptized fewer children but retained a correspondingly higher percentage of them, the rigorists *might* have a case. But from 1960 to 1985 confirmations declined even more dramatically, from 191,000 a year to 77,000, while Easter communicants, who remained above 2,000,000 till 1966, have now dropped to 1,624,000.[34] Greater rigour has solved nothing.

Yet still the possibilities remain. Still in many cases the seed sown in infancy brings forth fruit. There are parents, godparents, grandparents, Christian friends and other individuals to help in the work of nurture. There are day schools, Sunday schools, children's churches, uniformed organizations and a host of other groups. And behind all these, yet not restricted to them, there is the Holy Spirit. 'I practice indiscriminate baptism', said a URC minister recently, 'because I believe in the Holy Spirit'. We must prepare parents as carefully as we can. We must encourage the choice of suitable godparents. We must, as BEM urges, take more seriously the whole question of the Christian nurture of the baptized. But in the last resort it is because of our faith in the Spirit of God that we can still affirm that infant baptism looks forward to the child's growth as a Christian.

NOTES

1. Decree on Ecumenism 22, ET W. M. Abbott, *The Documents of Vatican II* (1966), p. 364.
2. *Ep.*98.7–10 (CSEL 34.528–33). ETs in Dods, ed., *Letters*, 2.20–23, and A. Hamman, *Baptism: Ancient Liturgies*, pp. 226–9.
3. *Summa Theologiae* 3.69–6, ed.cit., 57.38–41.
4. cf. Tertullian, *De Baptismo* 18, ed.cit., pp. 38f.; Ambrose, *De Sacramentis* 1.2.8 (CSEL 73.19); Caesarius of Arles, *Sermones* 71.2 (CC 103.301).
5. *Summa Theologiae* 3.71–1, ed.cit., 57.174f.
6. *Paraphrasis in Evangelium Matthaei*, praefatio, in *Opera Omnia*, ed. J. Leclerc (Leyden, 1703–6), 7.3v; cf. also J. D. C. Fisher, *Christian Initiation*, pp. 169f.; R. H. Bainton, *Erasmus of Christendom* (London, Collins, 1969), pp. 313f.; Canons of the Council of Trent, Of Baptism 14, in H. Denzinger, *Enchiridion Symbolorum* (Barcelona, 1963), no. 1627, p. 384.
7. *Ep.* 98.7–10, loc.cit.
8. n.244–47, ed. E. A. Lowe (Henry Bradshaw Society, vol. 58, 1920), p. 74; cf. E. C. Whitaker, 'The Baptismal Interrogations', *Theology* LIX (1956), pp. 103–12.

9. ed. M. Ferotin (Paris, 1904), col. 32.
10. *Sententiae* 14 dist. vi.6, ed. Collegium S. Bonaventurae (Quaracchi, 1916), 2.783.
11. *De Officiis Ecclesiasticis* 1.15 (PL 177.390).
12. *Contra Hereticos* 42 (PL 210.347).
13. *De Baptismo* 18, ed.cit., pp. 38f.
14. Chrysostom, *Baptismal Instructions* 2.15f., ET ed.cit., pp. 48f.
15. cf. Pseudo-Dionysius, *De Ecclesiastica Hierarchia* 7.3–11 (PG 3.568).
16. *Summa Theologiae* 3.67–8, ed.cit., p. 77.
17. Whitaker, *Documents of the Baptismal Liturgy*, p. 239; cf. also pp. 250f.
18. cf. Peter J. Jagger, *Clouded Witness* (Allison Park, PA, Pickwick, 1982), pp. 79–84.
19. *Constitutions and Canons Ecclesiastical* (1604) (1960), p. 11.
20. *Apostolic Christianity* (1898), pp. 319–35, cf. esp. pp. 326f.
21. *Holy Baptism* (1899), pp. 105–9.
22. *The Ministry of the Spirit*, ed. D. M. Paton (1960), pp. 193f.
23. Report no. 626, London, SPCK, 1939.
24 *Infant Baptism: History and Modern Practice*, Theology Occasional Papers New Series no. 1, London, SPCK, 1939.
25. XLI (1940), pp. 1–9.
26. *The Lambeth Conference 1948*, Part 1 (Resolutions) p. 50; Part II (Reports) pp. 106–15.
27. London, SPCK, 1949; cf. esp. pp. 26–30 and 36f.
28. *Baptism and Confirmation To-day*, London, SPCK, 1955, cf. esp. 1.10–16, 45f. There was also a minority report of a more rigorous nature.
29. *Baptism and Confirmation* (1959), p. 28.
30. *Of Water and the Spirit* (London, SPCK, 1976), pp. 160f.
31. Cited by the Bishop of Leicester, *Godparents*, GS Misc 202, p. 31.
32. General Synod, *Report of Proceedings* V (1974) 56.
33. *Believing in Baptism*, p. 149.
34. *1987 Church Statistics*, pp. 8f.

7

The Last Twenty Years

In 1947 work was started on a new body of canons to replace those of 1603. The first proposals on baptism made only minimal changes,[1] and the gradual amendment and enlargement of the proposals was a further reflection of the lively debate that had been taking place. Some of the provisions eventually agreed required changes in the rubrics of the Prayer Book before the canons could be legally promulged, as they were in 1969,[2] and in 1968 Parliament approved the Prayer Book (Further Provisions) (No. 2) Measure which gave effect to these changes. Copies of the 1662 Prayer Book printed since then (though not, strangely, the Prayer Book baptism service in *The Sunday Service Book* of 1988) have included the new rubrics instead of the original ones, and to check on the Prayer Book's present requirements it is important to refer to a recent copy and not an inherited one.

Looking at the rubrics and canons together, we can see eleven principal features in the present provisions.

First, it is 'desirable' that the minister shall 'normally' administer baptism 'on Sundays at public worship when the most number of people come together'. As promulged in 1969 the canon used 'from time to time' instead of 'normally' and spoke of 'at or immediately after public worship'; it is the only baptismal canon already to have been amended, and the stronger wording was substituted in 1978. The principle is admirable, provided of course that 'desirable' is not interpreted as 'essential' – baptism *only* at public worship. As against the obvious advantage 'that the congregation there present may witness the receiving of them that be newly baptized into Christ's Church, and be put in remembrance of

67

their own profession made to God in their baptism', there are two possible disadvantages. In some parishes the number of baptisms is still very large, and if even half were baptized at public worship the congregation's diet would become unbalanced. In other parishes the wider baptismal party may find it impossible to enter into the worship with even a minimum of understanding; sometimes they make this obvious, and neither they nor the regular congregation are edified. Perhaps the Roman Catholic provision is wiser. Here too baptism should take place on a Sunday whenever possible:

> It should be conferred in a communal celebration for all the recently born children, and in the presence of the faithful, or at least of relatives, friends and neighbours, who are all to take an active part in the rite.

It may even be celebrated during Mass 'so that the entire community may be present and the necessary relationship between baptism and eucharist may be clearly seen', but – a cautionary note – 'this should not be done too often'.[3]

Second, there is a requirement that 'Due notice, normally of at least a week, shall be given' before baptism. This does not relate to emergencies of course, and it is clearly right. The lesser notice of 1662 allowed no time for preparation and instruction, and no time to enquire about the sponsors. In practice, in most parishes 'at least a week' probably means a month.

Third, the rubric (at the beginning of the service for Private Baptism) that curates should admonish people not to defer their children's baptism longer than 'the first or second Sunday next after their birth' is deleted. The 1928 Prayer Book suggested 'the fourth, or at furthest the fifth, Sunday'. This was more realistic, and a slightly longer period might have been suggested today. But the total deletion of the rubric and the lack of an alternative suggestion is sad.

Fourth, the presence of the parents is now required: 'At the time appointed the godfathers and godmothers and the parents or guardians with the child must be ready at the font.' In spirit this again is right, and parents are normally present nowadays as a matter of course. But '*parent or* parents' might have been better, since a legalist might seek to refuse baptism if one parent requested it but the other was indifferent and refused to attend.

Fifth, the parents now have explicit responsibilities: 'The Minister shall instruct the parents or guardians of an infant to be admitted to Holy Baptism that the same responsibilities rest on them as are in the service of Holy Baptism required of the godparents.' These responsibilities are presumably only those listed in the Prayer Book's final exhortation, and Kuhrt is wrong to claim here a clear implication that the parents as well as the godparents must have been confirmed if their children are to be eligible for baptism.[4] Nonetheless the ignoring of the parents has always been the weakest point in the traditional procedures. They, more than the godparents, are in the best position to guide the child's Christian growth, and ideally 'They are the first to communicate the faith to their children'.[5] But while they now have the same responsibilities as the godparents and their attention should indeed be drawn to this, the baptism of their child does not depend on their acceptance of these responsibilities. There is a subtle but crucial distinction here, and to demand that the parents accept their responsibilities is to make the child's baptism dependent on their faith. But if the parents' acceptance is doubtful, the minister will need to be specially careful to ensure that the godparents are properly qualified.

Sixth, there is the provision that 'parents may be godparents for their own children provided that the child shall have at least one other godparent'. There is no qualification here like 'if need so require', and provided the parents fulfil the other qualifications they are fully entitled to be godparents for their children. They should be reminded, though, that if they choose to be godparents they are choosing to be the Church's ministerial agents and thereby are formally accepting their spiritual responsibilities for their child.

Seventh, there is the explicit statement that godparents 'shall be persons who . . . will faithfully fulfil their responsibilities both by their care for the child committed to their charge and by the example of their own godly living'. Parents *may* fulfil their responsibilities. Godparents *must*. The minister should draw the parents' attention to this, and the attention of the godparents too.

Eighth, there is the requirement that the godparents 'shall be persons who have been baptized and confirmed', though 'the Minister shall have power to dispense with the requirement of confirmation in any case in which in his judgement need so requires'. There can be no objection to the minister's power to dispense in particular cases. A godly but unconfirmed Methodist can make an excellent godparent, and it would be a foolish parish priest who rejected one. In general, though, they keyword here is 'need', and it is unfortunate that in many parishes dispensations are granted wholesale without the slightest regard to need. It might be better if there was an invariable insistence on two confirmed godparents, even if that meant that there were four or five godparents in all. Admittedly the provision of confirmed godparents still presents a problem for some parents, but this is more true in some areas than others, and if it meant that sometimes godparents had to be provided from the local congregation this could be a very good thing for, as we have seen, godparents are essentially the mouthpiece of the Church rather than the friends of the parents. Parental faith, or lack of it, is part of the 'givenness' of the situation, but godparents are a matter of choice and the Church speaks very clearly about the kind of people who should be chosen.

Ninth, there is the insistence (with the provision of appeal to the bishop) that

> No Minister shall refuse or, save for the purpose of preparing or instructing the parents or guardians or godparents, delay to baptize any infant within his cure that is brought to the church to be baptized, provided that due notice has been given and the provisions relating to godparents are observed.

70

In itself this insistence is admirable. The previous absolute prohibition of delay is now qualified by a recognition of the importance of preparation and instruction, and baptism is no longer available literally 'on demand'. But ministers must recognize that there are limits to preparation and instruction, and that they are not entitled to impose rigid tests of their own devising. The parents' right of appeal to the bishop is extremely important here.

Tenth, and linked with this, there is the absolute insistence that 'No minister being informed of the weakness or danger of death of any infant within his cure and therefore desired to go to baptize the same shall either refuse or delay to do so'. This is based on the 1603 canon, and is a reminder that in the last resort it is the principle of the necessity of baptism that takes precedence.

Lastly, there is the requirement that

> A minister who intends to baptize any infant whose parents are residing outside the boundaries of his cure, unless the names of such persons or of one of them be on the church electoral roll of the same, shall not proceed to the baptism without having sought the good will of the minister of the parish in which such parents reside.

For over a century now there have been churches with which particular families have established strong links and to which parents like to return for the baptism of their children even when they have left the parish. They may rarely worship at this church now, or indeed at any other, but they still think of it as 'their' church. Many priests are not unsympathetic here, especially when other members of the family still remain in the parish. They welcome even the tenuous link, and accept that semi-churched families often have a genuine, even religious, feeling for 'their' church. At the same time there are other churches where baptism is still administered very casually and which are especially popular with parents who want no demands and, as they would put it, no fuss. It is difficult to allow the former without in some way countenancing the latter, and the canon as promulgated is a careful compromise between the original proposal that clergy baptizing the children of non-parishioners should simply inform the parents' own priest after the event, and the stricter demand that baptism should always take place in the parents' own parish. The minister must now seek the goodwill (though not the consent) of the parents' own priest before proceeding to the baptism. Most clergy do this, and the system works well – especially when the parents themselves are encouraged to seek this goodwill. They are still able to have their baby baptized as they want in 'their' church, but they are brought into contact with their local parish priest who hopefully will be able to build on this contact. It is sad when the canon is ignored by the lazy priest, and equally sad when goodwill is refused by the rigorous.

Each of us, given a free hand to frame rubrics and canons, would have used different expressions at some point. But in general we have a proper adjustment of the details of our procedures to the pastoral needs of our times. Yet even before the new canons were promulgated moves were being made to go significantly beyond them and to alter the basis of baptism.

The trouble began with the Liturgical Commission's 1966–7 proposals which were eventually authorized as Series Two. Here, the opening address of the 1958 service becomes a rubric in which the requirement of a Christian upbringing is stated, and the priest is charged to ask the parents and sponsors whether, in three specific ways, they will provide this – although it is up to him whether he does this privately when the baptism is being arranged or publicly immediately before the service. A private asking of the parents is not unreasonable, but the compulsory addressing of questions to them as well as to the sponsors rings gentle warning bells, and these become a positive alarm-signal when they are again associated with the sponsors in 'The Decision' and the profession of faith. In 'The Decision', the priest says to both, 'Those who bring children to be baptized must affirm their allegiance to Christ and their rejection of all that is evil.' He reminds them that it is their duty 'to bring up these children to fight against evil and to follow Christ', and he asks them specifically, 'Do you turn to Christ?', 'Do you repent of your sins?' and 'Do you renounce evil?'. He then tells them, 'You must now make the Christian profession in which they are to be baptized, and in which you will bring them up', and to the three questions about Father, Son and Holy Spirit they reply, 'I believe and trust in him.'

The Commission realized that it was treading on dangerous ground here, and it offered a careful rationale of its procedures,

> In this service [child baptism], where the profession is made by the parents and sponsors, the question arises, 'Whose renunciation and faith is professed?' Is it the present renunciation and faith of parents and sponsors, or the future renunciation and faith of the child? We have tried to make the words of the service cover both views. The present renunciation and faith of the parents and sponsors is professed in their rejection of all that is evil, and their belief and trust in God. The future renunciation and faith of the child is affirmed by his baptism in this profession, in which it is the duty of the parents and sponsors to bring him up. In this way we have tried to retain the view expressed in 1662, that the child promises 'by his sureties' that he will renounce and believe, while placing the responsibility for the implementation of this promise upon the shoulders of those who made it on the child's behalf.[6]

The one thing lacking here, however, is even the slightest recognition that as far as the Church of England is concerned the linking throughout of 'parents and sponsors' is a total innovation. If parents had been *invited* to associate themselves with the sponsors in 'The Decision' and the profession of faith, that would have been excellent. If they had been linked with them on the assumption that they would normally wish to join them, but with a rubrical dispensation if they felt unable to, that too would have been fine. But in fact they are given no choice. What if only one can honestly say 'Yes'? What if neither can say 'Yes', but the child is sponsored by other members of the family who can? Series Two at a stroke seeks to make the Church of England more rigorous than Calvin, and implies very clearly that parental faith is an essential precondition of baptism.

Hardly had Series Two been authorized when the Ely

Commission was set up to consider the relationship between confirmation and admission to communion. It found itself discussing baptism as well, and its 1971 report showed a more open attitude than Series Two:

> We are, indeed, unanimously of the opinion that *the Church must never refuse Baptism if sincerely desired for their child by its parents or guardians.* Refusal of Baptism must, in the last resort, be the decision of the parents and not the responsibility of the parish priest, for we find it difficult to believe that any individual could make a child's right of Christian membership dependent upon his own assessment of the suitability of the child's parents or guardians.

They explained that by 'sincere desire' they meant 'a genuine longing that the child may enter into the Christian community where the grace of God is available through Christ'. It would be fittingly expressed by 'a willingness to ensure as far as possible the child's continual growth within the Church', and a proper criterion of it would be a readiness to receive such preparation as would enable them to take a 'sincere part' in the rite.[7]

The General Synod debated the Ely report in 1972, and the Standing Committee then commissioned Peter Cornwell to prepare a working paper as a basis for further debate; this was published in 1974. Cornwell pointed out that while in 1662 the godparents acted as spokesmen for the child, in Series Two they and the parents express their personal faith. The rite had eliminated the moral difficulty of vicarious promises but had accentuated the pastoral difficulty in that the promises were very explicit:

> The Church has to decide whether Infant Baptism should be administered to the children of parents who not only make the promises, but also show evidence that they will fulfil them, or whether Infant baptism should continue to be at the request of the parents, with the sole condition that they should make the promises.

To decide for the former would involve a change in church law, for there was a conflict between the Church's official policy as expressed in the new canons which supported baptism on request, and the Series Two promises which moved towards a more selective policy. But whichever policy the Church decided, this should determine the form of the promises in any future revision.[8]

Cornwell's analysis was misleading in that the main question the Church needed to decide was whether parents (as against godparents) should even be *required* to make the promises. The result inevitably was confusion. First, the Synod extended the authorization of Series Two with its rigorous requirements and then, the following day, passed what it regarded as an 'open policy' resolution declaring that it

> adheres to the view that Infant Baptism should continue to be available to the children of all parents who request it and are willing and able to make the requisite promises, and asks that the Liturgical Commission should note this expression of view, together with the requirements of Canon B.21, B.22 and B.23, in the framing of any new baptismal services.[9]

Despite the addition of the words 'and able' to the original motion, the motion as passed was still regarded as upholding baptism 'on request', and the decision whether they were 'willing and able' was to be that of the parents not of the parish priest.[10] In general this was good, though with its concentration on the parents, the view to which the Synod 'adhered' was not one which the Church had previously upheld!

The Liturgical Commission was now asked to prepare a modern-language Series Three service of infant baptism, and it issued its proposals in 1975. Here it recast the opening rubric on the duties of parents and godparents in the form of an address which closed with a direct question and the reply, 'I am willing'. It did not propose 'that this address should be mandatory in the course of the service, either in its use or in its terms', though this was not entirely clear in the layout of the service. It also made explicit that at 'The Decision' and the profession of faith the parents and godparents 'must answer for yourselves and for these children'. It explained that

> An assumption which underlies these questions, both in Series 2 and in this revision, is that infants are presented by parents and godparents who are believers and can answer in good faith the

questions which are put to them. We do not accept the view that these questions ought to be modified in such a way that they can be answered by people with no Christian convictions. If it is found that this raises difficulties on some occasions, when parents or godparents either will not answer the questions, or ought not to be encouraged to answer them, then the proper solution of the difficulty lies in the field of pastoral ministration and not of liturgical reform.[11]

The Commission was arguing curiously here since no one was seriously suggesting that baptismal questions should be answered by 'people with no Christian convictions'. The real problem was neither pastoral nor liturgical but doctrinal – the compulsory association of parents with godparents. The Commission referred to 'cases where parents who cannot conscientiously answer the questions themselves . . . are prepared to provide them with responsible godparents', and claimed that it was bound here by canon B.23. But this canon was irrelevant, and the Commission could have dealt with these cases perfectly well in a rubric or note.

In November 1976 the Synod compounded its confusions by passing a resolution with rigorist implications only two years after its previous 'open' resolution:

> That this Synod, endorsing the forms of interrogation in Series 2 and draft Series 3 Infant Baptism services, desires that there should be a re-examination of the conditions upon which infants are accepted for baptism.

This resulted in a brief but sound memorandum by E. G. Knapp-Fisher which gently upheld baptism on request on the traditional ground of the faith of the Church. Knapp-Fisher suggested that canon B.23 on godparents might be strengthened by the additional requirement that 'in every case one at least [of the godparents] shall be a regular communicant of the Church of England', and also that the opening address in the draft Series Three service should be enlarged to read, 'Parents and godparents, these children depend on you, *with the support of other members of this congregation*, for the help and encouragement they need'.[12] Sadly, the memorandum was never debated and the suggestions were not implemented.

In 1977 the Series Three proposals were reissued as part of a full series of Initiation Services, and here the provision that the opening address and its response should not be mandatory was deleted.[13] The services were authorized for use in 1979, and they passed into the Alternative Service Book in 1980. ASB thus completed the work which Series Two began, and on any straightforward interpretation it denies the Church's official teaching that infant baptism is not conditional on the faith of the parents. We can be grateful only that ASB is literally an 'alternative book', authorized for a limited period and lacking the fuller authority of the Prayer Book and canons. The tragedy is that in practice it is the only book that many people know (including many clergy), and if they seek the doctrine of the Church of England from this source they will get a woefully misleading impression of it. Thus Kuhrt, completely ignoring the Prayer Book, interprets the canons only in the light of ASB and declares that 'both the law and the liturgy of the Church of England require parents bringing a child to be baptized to be confessing, practising Christians themselves'.[14] But this is just not true. ASB exists only alongside, and subordinate to, the Prayer Book, and the official doctrine of the Church of England remains unchanged – that baptism is *not* dependent on the faith of the parents.

Since ASB reached its final form, there have been several further skirmishes. In 1980 the General Synod rejected a private member's motion that the words 'and able' be deleted from its 1974 resolution about parents and promises,[15] and in 1981 it asked for a debate on the role of sponsors, including their qualifications and selection. The Bishop of Leicester was then asked to prepare a report on godparents, which was issued in 1984,[16] and in 1985 a sensible proposal that there should invariably be one communicant godparent was narrowly defeated.[17]

Meanwhile in 1982 BEM had issued its warning against 'apparently indiscriminate baptism', and in 1986 the General Synod approved a response to BEM prepared by its Faith and Order Advisory Group:

People will come forward for baptism at a time when their response to the Gospel (or that of their sponsors) is incomplete. It is a delicate matter to judge who should be baptised and who deferred, as no response is without ambiguity. On the one hand the text is right to warn of the offence which the indiscriminate practice of baptism can cause, where admission to baptism is granted to those who do not seem to have given any evidence of wanting to be identified with Jesus Christ and his Church. On the other hand, baptismal discipline may be so 'over-discriminating' that those requesting baptism are required to provide unreasonable evidence of the authenticity of their faith. So called 'indiscriminate baptism' reflects a view of the Church as a 'mixed community'; a more rigorous policy emphasizes the 'gathered' nature of the Church.[18]

This carefully balanced response showed understanding of both positions, but rigorists deemed it 'ambivalent and unsatisfactory',[19] and in 1986 again a private motion was moved requesting 'as a matter of urgency' proposals which would respond to BEM's comments both on indiscriminate baptism and on the nurture of the baptized. In view of the pressure of time the motion was withdrawn, and at the Convocation of York in 1987 a similar motion was amended so that the reference to indiscriminate baptism was deleted. But at the Synod an official of the Convocation of York, in a confused speech which muddled parents and godparents, assured the mover that the 1974 motion about parents being 'willing and able' to make the promises – which at the time had been interpreted as upholding baptism 'on request' – was actually an expression of the Synod's mind to rule out indiscriminate baptism. He promised that consideration would be given to amending canon B.23 on godparents to take account of this motion about parents, and in 1988 it was confirmed that an amending canon would be introduced when time allowed.[20] Later in 1988 another private motion was moved calling attention to the concern about 'apparent indiscriminate baptism' expressed by BEM and 'increasingly shared by many people of differing theological persuasions in the Church of England'. Fortunately this was amended so that it also called attention 'to the concern felt by others over the theological implications of rigorous Baptism policies'.[21] There is now likely to be another debate in 1990.

Meanwhile, the Lambeth Conference in its Mission and Ministry report (though not in a formal resolution) has accepted BEM's judgement 'that indiscriminate infant baptism should not be practised':

It obscures the purpose of such baptism, not only from those who request it, but also from those many others who are doubtful about its propriety. Whilst we are aware of the vastly different contexts in which baptism is sought, we encourage the development of standards and guidelines for the preparation of parents and sponsors, with a view to a common discipline.[22]

How indiscriminate baptism obscures the purpose of baptism is not explained, and what Lambeth describes as indiscriminate baptism may really be careless rather than open baptism. Nonetheless, on the crucial issue of the demands which may properly be made on parents, most provinces of the Anglican Communion already require parents to make the promises with the godparents just as ASB does, although Australia has a happier rubric which states simply that 'It is desirable that the child's parents associate themselves with the godparents and make the answers with them'.

In the Roman Catholic Church the position is more complex. The Second Vatican Council decreed that the rite should be revised in order that, among other things, 'the roles of parents and godparents, and also their duties, should be brought out more sharply in the rite itself'.[23] The 1969 rite which was the result of this states that children are baptized 'in the faith of the church' which is proclaimed for them by their parents and godparents 'who represent both the local Church and the whole society of saints and believers'. Parents should prepare to take part in the rite with understanding, and it is 'very important' that they be present. Because of 'natural relationships', they have a more important ministry and role than the godparents. It is they who, accompanied by the godparents, present the child, and it is they who ask that the child be baptized and agree to accept the responsibility of training him 'in the practice of the faith'. The godparents then express their willingness to help the parents, and both together make the renunciations and the profession of faith. If one parent cannot make the profession, he may keep silent. All that is asked of him is that he arrange, or at least permit, that the child be instructed in the faith. If neither parent can profess the faith or undertake a Christian upbringing, 'it is for the parish priest, keeping in mind whatever regulations may have been laid down by the conference of bishops, to determine the time for the baptism'. The 1980 *Instruction* explains further that there must be assurances of an authentic education in Christian faith and life: if these are not really serious, 'there can be grounds for delaying the sacrament', and if they are clearly non-existent, 'the sacrament should even be refused' – though this refusal is really an 'educational delay'. But this is qualified by four other statements: first, the necessity of assurances is secondary to the necessity of baptism and the gift of its blessings; second, 'as a rule, these assurances are to be given by the parents or close relatives, although various substitutions are possible within the Christian community'; third, if the choice of godparents or the support of the community provide sufficient assurance, 'the priest cannot refuse to celebrate the sacrament without delay'; fourth, 'any pledge giving a well-founded hope for the Christian upbringing of the children deserves to be considered as sufficient'.[24]

Clearly Rome contemplates the possibility of delaying baptism for preparation and instruction, as does the Church of England and she now lays great emphasis on the parents and normally requires their full participation in the rite including the renunciations and the profession of faith. But what distinguishes Rome from most of our Anglican rigorists is that she still sees baptism as administered ultimately 'in the faith of the church' and that she wants to baptize infants if she possibly can. Hence her willingness in the last resort to accept assurances from close relatives, godparents or various substitutions. Anglican rigorists, however, believe that 'infants should be baptized not on the vague basis of "the faith of the church" but on the precise basis of the faith of the home',[25] and they wish to restrict baptism accordingly.

NOTES

1. *The Canon Law of the Church of England* (London, SPCK, 1947), pp. 122f.
2. *The Canons of the Church of England* (London, SPCK, 1969), Canons B21–23, pp. 17f. The canons are now issued in loose-leaf form, and amendments are supplied to subscribers.
3. *Rite of Baptism for Children* (Birmingham, Goodliffe Neale, 1970), paras. 8–14, pp. 5–7.
4. *Believing in Baptism*, p. 144.
5. Decree on the Apostolate of the Laity n. 11, ET Abbott, *Documents of Vatican II*, p. 502.
6. *Baptism and Confirmation* (1967), pp. 2f.
7. *Christian Initiation: Birth and Growth in the Christian Society*, GS 30 (1971), p. 35.
8. *Christian Initiation: A Working Paper*, GS 184, pp. 7–10. Cornwell was apparently unconvinced by the claim of the compilers of Series Two that both views were expressed in the rite. Be this as it may, he was right to point out that Series Two made new demands.
9. *Christian Initiation: A Discussion Paper*, p. 18. The reauthorization of Series Two was probably the result of its general merits as evidenced by its widespread adoption. The Synod was probably unaware of its contradictory attitudes.
10. ibid., p. 8.
11. *Alternative Services Series 3: Infant Baptism*, GS 225, p. 6.
12. *Infant Baptism: A Memorandum*, GS Misc 59, p. 11.
13. *Alternative Services Series 3: Initiation Services*, GS 343.
14. *Believing in Baptism*, p. 146.
15. Report of Proceedings XI (1980), 643–7.
16. *Godparents*, GS Misc 202.
17. *Report of Proceedings* XVI (1985), 336–53.
18. *Towards a Church of England Response to BEM and ARCIC*, GS 661 (1985), para. 45, p. 20.
19. Kuhrt, *Believing in Baptism*, p. 148.
20. *Report of Proceedings* XVII (1986), 992–4 and XIX (1988), 35.
21. ibid. XX (1989).
22. *The Truth shall make you free: The Lambeth Conference 1988* (London, Church House Publications 1988); Section report on 'Mission and Ministry' para. 192, p. 70.
23. Constitution of the Sacred Liturgy 67, ET Abbott, *Documents of Vatican II*, p. 160.
24. *Rite of Baptism for Children*, paras. 1–7, ed.cit., pp. 1–5; *Instruction* pp. 14–17.
25. C. O. Buchanan, *Policies for Infant Baptism* (Bramcote, 1987), p. 21.

8

Where Grove Goes Wrong

All Anglicans are agreed that parents have the most crucial role in the Christian nurture of their children, that they should be reminded of this and asked to accept it, that they should be invited to associate themselves with the godparents in making the renunciations and professions, and that they may properly choose to be godparents themselves. The trouble is that many are now *insisting* that parents accept their role and make their own Christian profession. They believe, in the words of Bishop Colin Buchanan, that

> There is no warrant to baptise any infants but those of whom the parents (or one parent) are members of the church, practising, believing, worshipping. Beyond that, no case for infant baptism can be made. The sacrament if administered in other cases is not invalid, but it is grossly misused and profaned.[1]

It was in 1972 that Buchanan started to produce the monthly *Grove Booklets*, and nobody else has produced anything to equal them. Those dealing with baptism have sought to offer a vigorous biblical defence of infant baptism, though this defence is vastly weakened in that it makes no mention of the Lord's requirement of new birth, it explicitly rejects the relevance of his welcome of the children and it also rejects the concept of the faith of the Church. In other words, Buchanan ignores or rejects the traditional core of the Church of England's apologia which calls so strongly for an open attitude and places such minimal stress on the status of the parents. In its place he offers eight lines of argument for infant baptism and claims that 'it is the work of a moment' to spot that each of them is 'an argument *limited to the children of believers*'. Each line, and the biblical case as a whole, 'relates to the standing in Christ of the parents, and only to that'.[2] But this is not so.

Buchanan's arguments are neither as strong nor (I believe) as biblical as the traditional ones, but the point here is that even these arguments do not, as he claims, justify the restriction of baptism in the way that he demands.

The first argument is from the covenant with Abraham and the rite of circumcision. Now most of us would attach fair weight to this as a general argument for infant baptism. Children in the Old Testament were incorporated into the people of God by circumcision. It is unlikely that God intended children in the New Testament to be worse off, and thus it is appropriate that they should be incorporated into God's people today by the new sign of baptism. This leaves entirely open which children should be incorporated, and this is something we would determine on other grounds. But Buchanan will not have this:

> The circumcising of Ishmael, then of Isaac, and of Esau and Jacob was dependent in each case upon the father's being the man of God to whom and through whom the promises of God were made and implemented. Any parallels with baptism must start from the status of the parents before God before proceeding to infer the propriety of the baptism of their children.

He lays great stress on these earliest generations, the sons first of Abraham and then of Isaac, and argues that we must work from the principles established here, and 'not from the later automatic inheritance of a place in the nation which is a large part of the administration of circumcision to infants in the rest of Jewish history.'[3] But why we must start here is not clear. Unless we want to see a perfect correspondence between baptism and circumcision (which nobody does), we relate to baptism only those aspects of circumcision which our doctrine of baptism suggests may be relevant. Buchanan's starting point, 'the status of the parents before God', seems not so much the starting point of his consideration of circumcision as a conclusion already reached on other grounds. It is just as reasonable, and on *my* other grounds preferable, to emphasize the broad understanding of Abraham's seed as included in God's promise and to emphasize, as Calvin did, the extension of the promise to a thousand generations.

The second argument is that baptism should be administered at the very beginning of the Christian life. For adults, Buchanan dislikes the catechumenate and stresses that in the New Testament adults were baptized at the point of conversion: 'Baptism is how the Lord and the Church make the man a convert – make him a Christian.' For infants, the question is: 'At what age is the child of a Christian home *first* entitled to be treated as a Christian?', and if he is to be treated as a Christian from birth it is proper that he should be baptized at birth; if he is not, his baptism will not be an initiation. But all this, Buchanan argues, 'relates only to those children who grow up *as believers from the start* within a believing home'. Here, however, the argument has subtly changed. With circumcision Buchanan was concerned with 'the status of the parents before God', and he might have argued now simply that the children of Christian parents are baptized because as covenant-children they *are* Christians. As it is, he goes on to speak of upbringing and environment, and of growth within a believing home. But a believing home is not easy to define. Buchanan speaks of 'members of the church, practising, believing, worshipping', but non-churchgoing parents may still teach their children to pray and still teach them something of God; they may still treat their children as Christians, and bring them up as such to the best of their ability. Nor are the parents the only influence. The child may be influenced by grandparents and godparents from the very beginning. Buchanan's apparently theological judgement is at least in part a sociological one, and a dubious one at that. Yet his initial premise stands. Baptism is indeed 'how the Lord and the Church make the man a convert – make him a Christian', and this is an excellent argument for open baptism. Parents request the baptism, godparents sponsor him in the faith of the Church, and the baptism follows quite properly.

Thirdly we have 'the evident baptism of whole households' which 'springs from, and depends upon, the baptism into Christ of the parent or parents of the household'. But the baptism of households may have included not just the householders' children and grandchildren, their literal offspring, but equally some nephews and nieces and even young slaves. If we cannot be sure that 'households' included children at all, we certainly cannot be sure that they included only the householders' own children. Clearly Buchanan's argument needs modifying here, and that infant baptism 'depends upon' parental baptism is an extraordinarily dangerous statement. But at a practical level we can accept that infant baptism normally springs from, and results from, the fact that the parents have been baptized, and it is rare indeed for baptism to be sought when neither parent is baptized. But baptized parents are far more common than 'members of the church, practising, believing, worshipping', and this third argument is again an argument for a thoroughly open baptismal approach.

The fourth and fifth arguments are linked with the second. In the first place church membership was enjoyed by young children in the New Testament, and although it is not absolutely provable that these children were from Christian homes, the fact of their baptism 'suggests strongly that their homes were Christian'. The argument here is somewhat circular, and the premise – that only children from Christian homes were baptized – dictates the conclusion. None the less we can gladly accept the conclusion, though it begs the question of what constitutes a Christian home. In the twentieth century a Christian home is as hard to define as is the 'believing home' of the second argument. This same ambiguity bedevils Buchanan's next argument about 'the impossibility of bringing up children in Christian homes in any way other than as Christians', an argument which as he rightly says 'is by definition an argument only related to the children of Christian parents'. Christian Parents are as hard to define as Christian homes. We know what the ideal is, but how far short can parents fall without ceasing to qualify as Christians? Or may not their own once-for-all baptism have a once-for-all significance which their subsequent lapsing can never negate?

The sixth argument is a new one: 'the conceding of the point that infant baptism should lead on to more or less immediate admission to communion'. There is something to be said for this concession, provided always that baptism is followed immediately by confirmation as in the Eastern Church. But in the present state of the debate Buchanan has conceded too much. It is one thing to state that infant baptism may quite properly lead on to more or less immediate admission to communion. Church history from 200 to 1200 would support such a statement, as would Eastern practice today. But it is another thing to state that infant baptism *should* lead to such admission. Subsequent church history has put a question-mark against this, and the mark has not yet been removed. Buchanan goes on to argue that the conceding of the point involves 'the presupposition that believing parents are taking their child to communion', but he does not state whether this is a weekly parish communion or an annual Easter communion. Nor does he countenance the possibility that believing grand-parents, godparents or neighbours may take the children. As in the second argument he assumes that the parents are the only influence.

Argument seven is from Acts 2.39, 'that the promise [of the gift of the Spirit through repentance, faith, and baptism] is "to you and your children"'. This, says Buchanan, 'assumes that the parents are being converted before their children come under consideration', and in its own context this is correct. But the quotation here needs to be completed: the promise is 'to you and your children and to all that are far off, every one that the Lord our God calls to him'. Once claimed, as it has been over many centuries in the West, it is valid, as Calvin put it, 'to a thousand generations'. Wherever infant baptism is sought in faith (not necessarily the faith of the parents), wherever – to quote Calvin again – 'the profession of Christianity has not wholly perished or become extinct', the promise remains. Once again we have an argument for a thoroughly open approach.

The final argument is from 1 Corinithians 7.14 and concerns 'the holiness of believers' children'. It is, as Buchanan admits, a 'somewhat ambiguous argument', and we can agree that 'insofar as it relates to infant baptism, it certainly relates only to the infants of believers, who are "holy"'. But Paul was writing here essentially about marital relationships. His reference to children, though relevant to his argument, was almost an aside. He was in no way enunciating a definitive doctrine of baptism, and it would be quite improper to draw any negative conclusions from his argument.

If we think now of Buchanan's arguments as a whole, we can accept that they have a cumulative weight (which is all he claims) in favour of the practice of infant baptism. But when we proceed to look at their implications for the scope of infant baptism, the restrictions which he claims as obvious are just not there. The first, third and seventh arguments imply at most that the parents are themselves baptized. The second, fourth and fifth concern upbringing and environment rather than in the strict sense 'the standing in Christ of the parents'. The sixth and eighth are only marginally relevant.

Details apart, there are two essential weaknesses in Buchanan's position. First, there is the restriction to parents of any influential role in the child's Christian growth. Grandparents, who we are told have kept the faith alive in Russia and who have no small influence in our own culture, do not figure anywhere, and godparents are similarly ignored. Noting that in medieval times the parents did not attend the baptism, he states that it is arguable that the moral role given to godparents in the Prayer Book 'was given only insofar as they were answering *in loco parentis*' and 'that the exhortations about upbringing in the BCP are really *for the parents*'.[4] It would be interesting to see the evidence for this argument. Meanwhile he states elsewhere that 'sponsors have no scriptural place and should not be thought to be undertaking anything about the child's upbringing'.[5] Neither in theology, law or pastoral practice, he claims, can much weight be placed on the requirement that they should be confirmed. There *may* be useful experience of providing godparents from the regular worshippers, even if unknown to the parents, but

they are certainly being wrongly used if they are thought to be representing the congregation's support for a Christian upbringing, as on the one hand infants should be baptized not on the vague basis of 'the faith of the church' but on the precise basis of the faith of the home, and on the other unless they are supporting those already known as worshippers their role is virtually impossible to fulfil anyway.[6]

Buchanan either does not see, or does not accept, the Prayer Book's clear understanding of godparents. But to those who do accept that view, their role remains important not least as a witness to the basis of baptism in 'the faith of the church'. The two things go together, and Buchanan has abandoned both.

Buchanan's second essential weakness is the over-confident distinction he draws between believer and unbeliever, between Christian and non-Christian. I am reminded here of the Franciscan who told me once that he 'hated the gospel'. It seemed an extraordinary statement from a man whose love for the Lord was beyond question, but what he meant was that he hated 'the gospel' as it had been appropriated to themselves by a narrow and exclusive group. Anglicans as a whole feel indignant if Roman Catholics restrict the name Catholic to themselves and deny it to others. Many of us feel equally indignant if particular groups imagine that they alone present 'the gospel' or that they alone are Christians. When we hear the cry, 'Baptism only for the children of Christian parents', we need to think carefully just what this means.

In the strictest sense there is only one Christian, and that is Our Lord himself. But in another sense every baptized person is a Christian. He may be a good Christian, a bad Christian, a devout Christian, a careless Christian, but he is still a Christian. 'Baptism only for the children of the baptized' still sounds exclusive in a way that infant baptism should not be, but most of us would accept it as a norm. It would be unusual if two unbaptized parents sought baptism for their child. If they did, I would want to be specially careful in their preparation and instruction, and specially careful too in checking the qualifications of the godparents.

Buchanan, however, demands more than the mere fact of baptism in the parents. They must be 'practising, believing, worshipping', and to be clearly distinguished as such they must be communicants.[7] Neil Dixon, a Methodist writer, agrees with him here,[8] and if more than baptism is indeed required it would be difficult not to agree. But all the baptized, whether communicants or not, are technically Christians, and if not themselves actively faithful, they are still formally 'of the faithful'. If we exclude their children, this can be only on the ground of the strictest covenant theology or because we have no hope whatever of their Christian upbringing. I believe that the theology here is wrong, and that the total lack of hope is faithless.

'Baptism only for the children of Christian parents' is also the plea of Kuhrt's recent book, *Believing in Baptism*. Kuhrt's tone is far more eirenic than Buchanan's, but he shares the same reformed theology. For him too, baptism is essentially a covenant sign for the children of believers, and where children are baptized whose parents are agnostics or indifferent 'baptism falls into disrepute, and can virtually cease to be *Christian* baptism at all.'[9] But very very rarely are we called on to baptize children when neither parent is baptized. The parents are still 'of the faithful'. If in practice they appear to be agnostic, this is where the godparents come into their own, and happily Kuhrt takes godparents more seriously than Buchanan does. As for indifference, the resentment usually caused by the refusal of baptism is a clear sign that the parents are not wholly indifferent. They are concerned at least about the baptism of their children even if they are not apparently concerned about their other Christian duties.

Kuhrt also argues that baptism must always be related to the preaching of the gospel and to the response of repentance and trust, and that there is confusion if the Church's mission, message and sacraments are seen to be at odds with one another. To each of these arguments I want to answer, 'Yes, but . . .'. Baptism is indeed related to the preaching of the gospel, but it is itself a 'visible word'. It is also related to the response of repentance and trust, but these are expressed very clearly by the godparents. Again, there is indeed confusion where mission, message and sacraments appear to be at odds with each other. But the mission is a universal one, the message is of prevenient love and grace so that 'while we were yet sinners Christ died for us' (Rom. 5.8), and the open administration of the sacrament to those who do not themselves reject it is a clear sign of this. There is consistency here rather than confusion. If there is confusion at all, it arises when church attendance is demanded of the parents as 'a good work' which then entitles their children to baptism. But perhaps we should abandon accusations of confusion, and remind ourselves instead of the paradox at the heart of the gospel. This is well expressed in the old evangelical dictum that admission to the kingdom is free but the annual subscription demands everything we have. Open baptism affirms the first of these truths, and it is for the on-going life of the Church to proclaim the second.

But Kuhrt sees a further drawback in general baptism: 'the large numbers inevitably lead to "private" baptisms, minimal instructions and widespread failure of any effective development of living faith'.[10] Yet there can be nothing wrong with large numbers as such; even the most open policy can hardly lead to the 3,000 who were baptized on the day of Pentecost! Admittedly large numbers may lead to baptism on other occasions than ordinary public worship, a hundred families a year cannot be prepared as thoroughly as two or three and the follow-up is much more difficult. But every pastoral situation has its problems. If there are problems with large numbers, there are equal – if different – problems in lack of numbers.

There are, of course, risks in baptizing more widely. Some people call themselves Christian, meaning 'decent', with the self-righteousness which is so characteristic of English 'religion', and we may suspect that they never give a thought to Our Lord from one year's end to another. If we accept them as Christians (as against Jews or Muslims) on the basis of their baptism, and if we then accept their children for baptism, we may well be taken for a ride no matter how carefully we seek to instruct and prepare. But risks are inevitable. Many of those who sought out Jesus were interested primarily in what they could get from him. Of the ten lepers who were cleansed, only one returned to give him thanks. Of his chosen twelve, one betrayed him. Of the thousands who heard him teach and were blessed by his words and deeds, there were only a hundred and twenty in the infant Church in Jerusalem. If Jesus was let down and betrayed, we can hardly complain if we are.

But sometimes there are joyous surprises from those of whom we expect little, and we must be very cautious in speaking of the insincerity or lack of faith of parents and godparents. If parents seem insincere, we only make matters worse by demanding of them an explicit profession of faith which we have not demanded before. If godparents seem insincere, we may again be to blame if we have not striven to ensure that some at least have been confirmed. If they really are insincere, their insincerity is tragic, but sometimes we mistake ignorance for insincerity, and in looking for the fulness of faith which is not there we fail to see the genuine measure of faith which is there.

In their 1939 protest, the clergy of Poplar wrote,

> Normally, the parents of the child are not practising Christians; neither are the sponsors . . . It is obvious to the officiating priest that the questions put to them, and the answers and promises made, mean nothing whatever . . . He cannot help feeling that he is lending himself to the performance of a solemn farce.[11]

Every clergyman has shared this feeling at one time or another. Yet sometimes our feelings are exaggerated. Very rarely have I encountered parents and sponsors for whom it is 'obvious' that the questions and answers mean 'nothing whatever' – and even here I ought to say 'it appears' rather than 'it is obvious'. Frequently the parents and sponsors do not mean by their answers all that I would like them to mean, but this is very different from saying that they mean 'nothing whatever'. To judge in this way is not helpful. None of us can boast that we always mean all that we should in our prayers and devotions. It is not that we are guilty of deliberate dishonesty (though we probably are at times). It is rather that even the simplest prayers and professions of faith have a depth of meaning and implication far greater than we normally perceive.[12]

The Prayer Book contains many instructions, most of which most people ignore. But to carry out some duties is better than to carry out none, and one of the few instructions which most people have taken seriously throughout the centuries is the instruction to have their babies baptized. Of course this has been linked up with dubious theology about the fate of

91

unbaptized infants, with folk religion of the crudest kind, with ideas of naming and registration, with social convention and all the rest of it. But it is not sentimental to suggest that it has also been linked – and still is – with 'a stirring of religious awareness aroused by the mystery of birth and a new life; a desire to give thanks, and to do their best for the helpless infant now entrusted to them'.[13] The Church has told them that that 'best' was baptism. They have brought their children as they were told to, and the language of the service has made it plain that they had acted rightly. Their descendants today are rarely aware of the latest theological currents. They bring their children now in the same spirit. They are bewildered if it is suggested to them that they are wrong to do precisely what they have been told to do. They are resentful too if they are told that they are not qualified to have their children baptized. It is their children for whom they are seeking baptism, and they have never been told before that the child's right to baptism depends on their own spiritual state. A very small minority of parents will be resentful of anything, even the requirement of a single preparation meeting or a gentle reference to the qualifications of godparents. We cannot entirely avoid this, but we can usually accomplish much more by a positive approach than a negative one. The priest whose initial response is, 'Yes, we shall be delighted to baptize your baby, and . . .' can often lead the parents much further than one who responds with suspicion and quickly imposes conditions.

That the priest with 'the cure of souls' should seek to assess the spiritual state of his people is entirely proper. But he must do this with great humility and in full recognition that his assessments are tentative and his judgements fallible. He must remember that if Jesus reproved those of little faith, he also spoke of the power of any faith, even 'faith as a grain of mustard seed' (Matt. 16.20). In many people faith is inchoate and confused. They do not deal easily in words, and they cannot express it well. But it is rarely if ever wholly absent in those who bring their children. It is the pastor's job not to devise elaborate hoops and hurdles, but to recognize the 'mustard seed' of faith and through preparation and after-care to encourage its growth.

In all this, though, we must bear in mind not only the importance of 'a sincere desire' on the part of parents that their infants should grow up as Christians and members of the Church, but also the comment of the Ely Report on this desire:

> The danger must be avoided of interpreting this desire in intellectual terms: looking for theological understanding of the Christian system of belief; or in ecclesiastical terms: looking for regular churchgoing . . . on the part of parents in the case of an infant. There may be some persons who sincerely want to identify themselves with a group living in Christ's spirit but may yet be unable to recognise this in the local Sunday congregation in Church.[14]

These last words are a judgement on us all. They are a judgement on lazy Christians who are 'unable to recognise' because they are unwilling to look. But they are also a judgement on the Church as a whole because that recognition is often extremely difficult even when people are looking very hard.

A Church which baptizes infants widely will never have clearly defined boundaries. But that is no bad thing, for there are terrible dangers in dividing people into Christians and non-Christians on any basis other than the objective one of baptism. It is always arbitrary, and it does not allow for the movement of people – and within people – that takes place every day. There is an encouraging movement of adults into the Church, as evidenced by the 10,000 adult baptisms which take place each year, an average of 25–30 each day. There is a sadder movement away from active church life, as evidenced by the vast numbers of lapsed communicants. But these lapses are often gradual, and no one can tell whether they will prove temporary or permanent. Newly-confirmed youngsters may be regular in their communion for a few months, and then appear only at Christmas and Easter; but they may become regular communicants again when they are preparing for marriage or when their children are growing up. They may lapse again in middle life, but return once more in their seventies. Sometimes even people whom their clergy regard as wholly committed feel (however wrongly) that they just cannot get to church for long periods when they are caring for sick relations or when their children are very young. Some drift away altogether, but others return as full of enthusiasm as ever.

A Church which baptizes infants widely will also include, even in its active ranks, a fair number of the half-committed, and many of its members seem to be stuck in this position all their lives. Most Anglicans are thoroughly familiar with this Church and need no further description of it. Yet the Church which welcomes and accepts people just as they are also calls them to fuller and deeper commitment and actually leads many of them to such commitment. This is exactly what Jesus did. And because it dare not take itself too seriously, this Church is also well placed to look beyond itself to that wider rule of God in the world which the Church exists to proclaim, interpret and extend but which it must never identify simply with its own life.

At the moment, infant baptism is one of the fronts on which a battle is being fought for the soul of the Church of England. It is a battle about whether we are to remain a broadly-based Church or degenerate into a narrow and exclusive one. If the Church of the half-committed is saddening at times (and no priest will deny this), the alternative, the Church of the elect, is terrifying. Here there is steadfast allegiance to truth as it is conceived, but it is rarely recognized that this is never more than a partial understanding of truth. The questioning are suspect, the unsound are excluded, the lines and possibilities of growth are all laid down in advance, and there is no scope for others to grow in different ways. Sin is rigorously resisted and the habitually sinful are rejected, but obvious sin, usually of the sexual kind, receives most of the strictures and the more subtle forms of sin, which persist in us all, are unrecognized or unacknowledged.

The visible Church has always been a mixed company, and every attempt to establish a 'pure' church has foundered horribly. 'Let both grow together till the harvest' (Matt. 13.30) was the Lord's injunction. Only then will people (including ourselves) be seen for what they really are. Until then we judge and discriminate at our peril.

NOTES

1. *Baptismal Discipline*, p. 9.
2. *Policies for Infant Baptism*, p. 3.
3. *Baptismal Discipline*, p. 8, and *A Case for Infant Baptism* (Bramcote, 1984), p. 12.
4. *The Liturgy for Infant Baptism (Series 3)*, pp. 23f.
5. *Baptismal Discipline*, p. 20.
6. *Policies for Infant Baptism*, p. 21.
7. *Baptismal Discipline*, p. 17.
8. *Troubled Waters* (London, Epworth, 1979), pp. 160–7.
9. *Believing in Baptism*, p. 134.
10. ibid., p. 136.
11. *Infant Baptism: History and Modern Practice*, p. 27.
12. For a penetrating analysis of what parents may mean, and for much more of relevance to the present chapter, cf. Wesley Carr, *Brief Encounters* (London, SPCK, 1985), pp. 38–41, 44f. and 63–85.
13. B. S. Moss, *Crisis for Baptism*, p. 23.
14. pp. 27f.

A Liturgical Postscript

I have written this book with a single purpose – to plead that our attitude to infant baptism should be as open as in the past. At times I have been critical – of other writers, synodical resolutions and current trends. But essentially I have sought to justify my five positive assertions:

1. Infant baptism should still be regarded as the norm here in England.

2. Infant baptism speaks not of original guilt but of God's prevenient grace.

3. Infant baptism should reflect the welcome which Jesus gave to the children.

4. Infant baptism is administered in the faith of the Church.

5. Infant baptism looks forward to the child's growth as a Christian.

The baptismal liturgy has not been my main concern, but this liturgy and the rubrics that accompany it both express our attitudes and also form them. I have had to touch on liturgy quite a lot, and at times I have again been critical. At most points of criticism, however, I have suggested brief amendments and I now want to gather these up. I am not of course offering a total critique of the rites, and I mention only those aspects which relate to my basic themes.

The Book of Common Prayer

The rubrics (amended in 1968) are sensible, and the rite itself has great merits. There is the gospel story of Jesus and the children, and there is Cranmer's splendid exhortation based on this. There is also the fact that the questions are addressed to the godparents, and while most priests would be glad if the parents joined in the answers, these answers are not formally required of the parents. Baptism is clearly in 'the faith of the church'.

The great weakness of the Prayer-Book rite has always been its Augustinian emphasis on our being 'born in sin' and on the child's deliverance from the wrath of God. In Series I, following 1928, this emphasis was reduced. The formal authorization of Series I has now lapsed, but in January 1988 the House of Bishops, having considered customary variations in the use of the Prayer Book,

> agreed in regarding the continued use, where well established, of any form of service which has, at any time since 1965, been canonically authorised (notwithstanding the fact that such authorisation was not renewed after it lapsed) as not being 'of substantial importance', within the meaning of Canon B 5.4.

In other words, where the Series I service was previously in use, as for example in parishes which used *The Shorter Prayer Book*, the minister 'in his discretion' may continue its use. For our purpose, the Prayer Book rite in its Series One form is admirable, and a modern-language version as an alternative to the ASB rite would be enormously useful.

Series Two

At present the order of the Series Two rites is Adult Baptism and Confirmation; Adult Baptism; Infant Baptism; Confirmation. It would be better if this order were amended so that Infant Baptism was placed first to indicate that, for us, this is still the normative rite.

In itself the Series Two rite is a thoroughly usable one, and those who have used it over many years would almost certainly agree that 'it works'. The reference to Jesus and the children is retained, and the rite in general is less verbose than the Prayer Book and Series One.

There are, however, two great weaknesses, and the first is the apparently mandatory association of the parents with the godparents at every point. The *parental* turning to Christ, repentance of sin and renunciation of evil is an apparently integral part of the rite, as also is their making of their Christian profession. The second weakness is the emphasis on conditions to be fulfilled rather than on God's acceptance. The opening rubrics, even though not read in the service itself, impart a totally different feel from that imparted by Cranmer's exhortation on the gospel story.

Both these defects, however, could be easily remedied. In the first place, the questions could be addressed as in the past to the godparents, with a rubric as in the Australian book, 'It is desirable that the child's parents associate themselves with the godparents and make the answers with them.' Secondly, there could be an exhortation similar to Cranmer's at an early point in the service. It is not that the requirements specified in the rubric are wrong; it is rather that they distort the balance and that the balance needs to be put right.

If these two simple amendments were made, the objections to Series Two would be removed at a stroke.

The Alternative Service Book

ASB is derived more from Series Two than from the Prayer Book, and my criticisms of Series Two apply equally to ASB: the order of the rites should be amended, the association of the parents with the godparents should be presented as desirable rather than mandatory, and the balance of the service should be redressed so that there is a proper emphasis on God's action and God's acceptance.

At two points, however, ASB has gone beyond Series Two and thus stands in need of further amendment. First, the rubrical requirements of Series Two have been changed into a formal statement which concludes with a direct question to which parents and godparents must reply 'I am willing'. This is objectionable on three grounds: it appears to make the baptism conditional on the parental response; it duplicates the decision and the profession which come later in the service; and it further distorts the balance of the service. It would be much better if the statement and question were omitted, or if necessary recast in rubrical form, and the service were to begin with the positive proclamation, 'The Lord is loving to everyone' (sec. 44).

The second sad feature is the omission of all reference to Jesus and the children. This reference should certainly be reinstated, with an exhortation similar to Cranmer's. This reinstatement would do a great deal to restore the balance of the service which at the moment is sadly lacking.

In one sense my suggested amendments both to Series Two and to ASB are very small and the bulk of the services would not be affected at all. But the rubrics are like the small print of a legal document; one is tempted to ignore them, but a single word can make a crucial difference. I believe that my suggested amendments to both rubrics and rites would make just such a difference. At the moment we are being led astray by bad theology into a sad sectarianism. These amendments, based as I believe on sounder theology, would help to recall us to our continuing vocation to be the Church of England.

Index of Biblical References

Index of Names

Alan of Lille 56
Aland, K. 8, 15, 31, 39
Allen, R. 59f
Ambrose 65
Augustine 17–19, 42–4, 52, 54f, 97

Bailey, D.S. 52
Bainton, R.H. 65
Barclay, W. 38
Bausch, W.J. 21, 26f
Bicknell, E.J. 20–2
Boniface 42, 54, 56
Bradshaw, P.F. 35
Brockett, L. 27
Bromiley, G.W. 27, 39, 52
Bucer, M. 32, 37–40, 45f, 48, 53
Buchanan, C.O. 36, 81–9
Bullinger, H. 32, 39, 46, 52

Caesarius of Arles 65
Calvin, J. 32, 39, 45f, 48, 73, 83, 86
Carr, W. 95
Cartwright, T. 49
Chrysostom 23
Cornwell, P. 74f, 81
Cranmer, T. 32, 36–8, 97–9
Cullmann, O. 25, 31–3
Cyprian 8

pseudo-Dionysius 43
Dix, G. 9–11, 52
Dixon, N. 88

Eastman, A.T. 12f, 15
Erasmus 55, 65

Fairweather, E.R. 52
Fisher, J.D.C. 39f, 52f, 65

Goode, W. 40, 47
Green, M. 36, 39

Habgood, J.S. 63
Hart, G.W. 20, 36, 39
Henson, H.H. 4, 58–60
Hermann of Cologne 40, 45
Hippolytus 8, 42
Hooker, R. 49
Horton, W.D. 37

Inchley, J. 27, 40

Jagger, P.J. 27, 66
Jasper, R.C.D. 35
Jeremias, J. 8, 15, 30f, 33, 38f
Johansson, N. 38

Kavanagh, A. 9, 13, 27
Kingdon, D. 37
Knapp-Fisher, E.G. 76
Knox, J. 53
Kuhrt, G. 14, 64, 69, 77, 81, 89f

Langland, W. 19
Leeming, B. 27
Luther, M. 32, 39, 41, 44

Maurice, F.D. 24f, 27f
Moberly, G. 52, 58, 63
Moss, B. 4, 7, 14–16, 27, 64, 95
Motyer, J.A. 36, 39

Origen 8
Osborn, R.R. 7, 36

Parker, M. 48
Pawson, D. 37
Peter Lombard 56
Pocknee, C.E. 29, 39

101

Index of Subjects

103

Index

Index